Jewish Cemeteries of Devon:

Exeter, Torquay & Paignton and Plymouth

Helen Fry

First Published: 2012
Copyright: Helen Fry 2012
Second Edition: 2013

The right of Helen Fry to be identified as the Author of this work has been asserted in accordance with the Copyrights, Designs and Patents Act 1988.

All rights reserved. No part of this e-book may be reprinted or reproduced or utilized in any form or by any electronic, mechanical or other means, now known or hereafter invented, including photocopying and recording, or in any information storage or retrieval system, without the permission in writing from the Author or her Agent.

Website: www.helen-fry.com
Agent: Steph Ebdon, The Marsh Agency Ltd, London

Copyright and Design of e-book cover: Edward Fry

CONTENT PAGE

Introduction

Section 1   Old Jewish Cemetery, Exeter

Section 2   New Jewish Cemetery, Exeter

Section 3   Torquay & Paignton

Section 4   The Hoe, Plymouth

Section 5   Gifford Place, Plymouth

Further Reading

About the Author

INTRODUCTION

This book is intended to be a helpful reference for family historians and Jewish genealogists searching for Jewish roots in Devon. No extensive list of Jewish burials in all five Jewish cemeteries of Devon currently exists and therefore this book provides the first comprehensive catalogue. Over a period of nearly fifteen years the author has researched, photographed and catalogued the burial sites; expanding on the research of scholars before her, like Dr Berlin and Rabbi Dr Bernard Susser. Without their early vital work many of the cemeteries could not be catalogued as well as they have been here because sadly today there are too many headstones which are partially, or totally, illegible. In two of the Devon Jewish cemeteries (Exeter and Torquay & Paignton) every single extant headstone was individually photographed by the author during the 1990s, making it currently the most comprehensive such photographic archive. Today, over twenty years later, many of these headstones are also now eroded and illegible. Thus, but for the early work, their inscriptions would be lost. Each section below begins with a very brief overview of the particular cemetery history, followed by a list of those buried there. Some of the early tombstones from 1740s onwards did not survive into the 20th century and have therefore never been catalogued. Even so there are somewhere in the region of 1,500 burials listed in total. In some cases it has been difficult to ascertain exact rows of graves and therefore the original numbering by Dr Berlin and Rabbi Dr Susser has been retained here. For a more detailed study of the history of the development of the cemeteries it is suggested that reference is made to other local Jewish community histories.

Devon has a long and rich Jewish history of settlement in the county that stretches back nearly three hundred years to the early 1720s. Exeter actually boasted an important Jewish centre in the Medieval period prior to the expulsion of Jews from England by Royal Edict in 1290. After Jews were readmitted to England under Oliver Cromwell in 1656, it took around sixty years before Jews settled in the two main Devon 'capitals' of Plymouth and Exeter. They came, not primarily as pedlars and hawkers, but skilled tradesmen and merchants: silversmiths, watchmakers, snuff merchants and clothiers. The Naval connections with Plymouth would be far-reaching with no less than forty Navy Agents operating in the area at one time. A viable worshipping community was established in Plymouth and Exeter by the 1740s such that both looked to acquire a burial ground around twenty years before a synagogue was built. Plymouth is today proudly the oldest Ashkenazi synagogue in the English-speaking world and has just celebrated its 250th anniversary, having been built in 1762. Following close behind is Exeter whose synagogue was built a year later in 1763 and is the second oldest synagogue in the English-speaking world. These two beautiful Georgian synagogues now have listed status and represent a pure gem in Anglo-Jewish heritage. However it would not be until the 1930s and the outbreak of the Second World War before a community was established in Torquay and incorporated Paignton too. This met the needs of the evacuees and refugees who came to live there during the wartime. Sadly with the decline in numbers over subsequent decades, the Torquay Hebrew Congregation is now defunct. Only the cemetery in Paignton survives to attest to Jewish life in the 'English Riviera' and a small archive of documents in the Devon Record Office. Exeter and Plymouth Hebrew Congregations still hold regular services and their synagogues can be visited by appointment.

SECTION 1
OLD JEWISH CEMETERY EXETER

The original Jewish cemetery is located in Magdalen Street and can still be visited today by contacting the community. It was acquired in 1757, although the earliest extant tombstone dates to 1807. It is surrounded by an 18th century red brick wall and entrance through an arched gateway which are both Grade II listed. Here are the graves of Moses Horvitz Levi (1754-1837), Minister of the congregation for twelve years and Solomon Aarons who died in 1864 at the great age of 102. Also minister Rev. Abraham Rosenberg who died in 1913. Here too rests Hannah, daughter of Moses Vita Montefiore and relative of Sir Moses Montefiore. There are a number of graves for members of the families of Gabrielson, Lazarus, Alexander, Levy, Aarons and Samuels; and the only Commonwealth War Grave of Pilot Officer H D Abrams, Air Observer of the Royal Canadian Air Force. The ground has seen around 200 burials since its opening in 1757.
Today the old Jewish cemetery has just one burial plot remaining which has been reserved for a life-long member of the community.

Other Jewish burials now take place in a special section at the Exwick Municipal Cemetery. A more detailed history of the old burial ground can be found in the author's book on the history of the Jews of Exeter published by Halsgrove in 2013.

Against the wall - next to the chapel:

1. 1827, ISAAC (?)

Front Row

2. No name. Surface illegible: all Hebrew. 12 lines. 1807

3. JACOB DAVD, 15 December died 15 December 5602 [1842], aged 55

4. JOHN JACOBS, 1911

Against Left Wall

5. Indistinct. Sunk in earth. No date

6. 1839: HANNAH relict of Moses Ancona, and daughter of the late Moses Vita Montefiore. 25 April 5599, aged 71

ROW 2

7. Grave of B.L. died [?]

8. LEVY ALEXANDER, 21 November 5615/1855, aged 99 years and 7 months

9. FANNY ALEXANDER, died 29 September 5612/1852, aged 89

10. BETSY EZEKIEL, relict of Henry Ezekiel, died 16 September

5611/1851, aged 68

11. PRISCILLA ELLEN MYERS, died June 1852, aged 17

12. ELIZABETH LEVY, wife of late Emanuel Levy, died 28 September 1852, aged 91 and 9 months

13. ISAAC SOLOMON, died 22 June 5614/1854, aged 82 years

(Apart)

14. SAMUEL LEVY, 1824, Hebrew only on the tombstone, design of a ewer and basin

ROW 3

15. BETSEY LAZARUS, wife of David Lazarus, 12 July 1848, aged 44

16. ESTHER JACOBS, sister of Jacob Jacob of this City, aged 60, died 9 April 5608/1848

17. HYMAN COHEN of this City, died 14 April 5607/1847, aged 78, design of hands of Cohen on the tombstone

18. PHOEBE COHEN, died January 1848, aged 80

19. ELIZABETH DAVIS, died 20 January 5608/1848, aged 48

20. ELIEZER LAZARUS, died 26 Heshvan 5605, 4 November 1845, aged 56

ROW 4

Two mounds of graves, no headstones

21. CATHERINE LAZARUS COHEN, died 1840, aged 69

22. MIRIAM DAVIS, died November 1838, aged 52

23. AMEILIA EZEKIEL, daughter of Abraham Ezekiel, 13th Sivan 1839, aged 60 [death certificate says 6th June = 23rd-24th Sivan]

24. CATHERINE EZEKIEL, daughter of Abraham Ezekiel, died 3 July 1837, aged 69

25. JUDITH PHILLIPS, died 28 December 559[?], aged 89 (?)

26. (Small, indistinct), Hebrew poem. No date

ROW 5

27. RACHEL DAVIS, died 10 Eyor 5597/1835, aged 84

28. AARON SAMUEL PARIS, 1836, erected by lamenting parents.

29. LAZARUS COHEN, died 14 Tishri Motzei Shabbos5595/1836, aged 71

30. JULIA LAZARUS, wife of Eleazar Lazarus of this City, died 2nd Av 5596/1836

31. JACOB JACOBS, died 17 December 1836, aged 57

32. HENRY EZEKIEL, 10 November 5596/1836

33. JUDITH DAVIS, 10 January 1837, aged 73 years

(2 grave spaces)

34. SAMUEL MARKS, son of Joseph Marks, 1870, aged 12

ROW 6

35. MOSES JOHNSON, died 26 August 5592/1832 aged 76

36. SARAH SOLOMON, died 29th May 5592/1832 aged 82

37. MOSES HORVITZ LEVI, Minister of this Congregation 42 years, died 5594 [1834], aged 80

38. CATHERINE LEVY, wife of Moses Levy, died 7 October 1834, aged 59[?] years

ROW 7

39. (Small, indistinct) DAVID COHEN, son of Andrew and Lavinia Cohen [no date]

40. MOSES ALEXANDER, 1835, aged 8 months

41. (No English) 1829

42. Same gravestone shape as No.40 and no English, 1832, mother of Baruch Jonas.

43. 1831, aged 68 (No English), Probably ABRAHAM COHEN brother of Lazarus Cohen

ROW 8

44. Sacred to the Memory of DOROTHY LYONS, died 13 February 5585/1825, aged 52

45. (No English), 5587/1827

46. JULIET LEVY, beloved wife of Gershon Levy (of Guernsey), aged 72, died 13 August 5586/1826

47. BARENT GOMPERTZ, died 9 September 5584/1824 (Altar Tomb).

The marble top chipped off.

ROW 9

48. LAZARUS MOSES JOHNSON, died 5581/1821, aged 86

49. SAMUEL BENEDICT, 5581/1821, aged 81

50. GERSHON LEVY of Guernsey, 5582/1822

51. ISRAEL MYERS, 1827, aged 14

ROW 10

52. (Indistinct) 1816

53. NANCY LAZARUS, wife of Moses Lazarus, died Sunday 2[0?] Shevat, 1810

54. MOSES LAZARUS of this City, died 2nd Adar 5571/1811

55. (Indistinct) 1816

Five further tombstones indecipherable

A tombstone apart: with 15 Hebrew lines, indistinct

ROW 11 [From back]

56. ROSINA ELSNER, wife of Solomon Elsner, 1861

57. HARRIET JACOBS, 1862

58. DAVID LAZARUS, 1862

59. SOLOMON AARONS, aged 102, 1864

60. FANNY AARONS, 1861

61. 1861

62. ISABELLA MYERS, wife of B. Myers, died November 1859, aged 56

63. NAPHTALI SOLOMON, died 15th March 5618/1858, 85 years

64. FOGEL SOLOMON, 31 October 5617/1857, aged 80 years

65. FOGEL beloved infant of Myers and Deborah Solomon, died 3 May 1859, 3 weeks and 13 days

66. LOUISA SCHULTZ, 1866, aged 74

67. CATHERINE AARONS, 1864

68. ANN JACOBS, died 27 Tamuz 1864, aged 60[?] years

ROW 12

69. LAURA GABRIELSON, died 12 March 1937, aged 55

70. HARRIET GABRIELSON, died 22 February 1924, aged 78, wife of Morris Gabrielson

71. SIMON SILVEREMAN, 25 July 1919, aged 78

72. EUGENE JOEL, died 14 February 1918, aged 85

From Back

ROW 8

73. FANNY MILCAH SOLOMON, daughter of Myers and Deborah Solomon, died aged 11 years and 4 months, 27 Tamuz 1871

74. HENRY M HYNES, aged 55 [?], died 29 May 1871

75. DAVID FRANKLIN, 1869, aged 84

76. HENRY LAZARUS, 1867 aged ?

ROW [?]

77. JONAS WALTER, died 1888 aged 65, Brother of Catherine and Henry Walter and Ann Cohen of Lyme Regis and New Oxford Street, London

78. GUSTAVE GITTLESON, son of Charlotte and Samuel Gittleson, died 24 August 1893, aged 8 months

79. MORRIS GABRIELSON, died 5 January 1905, aged 60

80. EMANUEL JACOBS, died 6 June 1903, aged 83

81. ALEXANDER ALEXANDER, died 22 February 1887, aged 83

ROW 3

82. AARON JOSHUA NUNEZ (Indistinct), 1846[?]

83. (Indistinct)

84. FLORENCE MIRIAM GOODMAN, died 1897, aged 34

85. HARRIET AARONS, died 22 January 1897, aged 64

86. PRISCILLA ZAMOISKY, died April 1908, aged 87

87. EVERETTA GLYNN, died Adar 1910 [14 March 1910], aged 34

ROW 2

88. AARON SOLOMON, died 5610 [1850]

89. ELIZABETH ABRAHAM, 24 October 5503, aged 51

ROW 7

90. AARON ISRAEL, died 20 September 1874, aged 72

91. AARON AARONS, died 1874, aged 48

92. LOUIS SCHULTZ, died 19 December 1873, aged 94

93. KATHERINE ABRHAMS, wife of Joseph Abrahams, died 23 September 1873, aged 84

ROW 6

94. LAWRENCE A. ALEXANDER, died 13 Sept 1881, aged 43

95. ABRAHAM SOLOMON PALMER, died 13 March 1879, aged 85

96. BETSEY JONAS, died 25 November 1878, aged 85

97. ESTHER JACOB, widow of Jacob Jacob, died 21 October 1874, aged 85

SOLOMON CAPPELLE, died September 1874, aged 35, location of grave no longer known, probably never had a headstone

ROW 5

98. BARNET JONAS, 23 January 1885, aged 79

99. JONAS LEVY, died 19 February 1884, aged 85

100. ALFRED KENNARD, died 17 December 1883, aged 36

101. (No English). BENJAMIN SON OF JOEL who died at the ripe old

age. His days were lengthened to 82 years. He died on the first day of the week and was buried on the same day 27th Shevat 5643 [1883]

102. ANDREW GEORGE JACOB, born at Falmouth, Cornwall, died at Exeter, March 1900

103. GOLDA RAPHAEL, wife of Aaron Raphael, died 11 August 1915

104. REV. ABRAHAM ROSENBERG, Minister of the Hebrew Congregation of Exeter, died 12 May 1913, aged 61

ROW 1

105. AARON RAPHAEL, died 12 January 1918, aged 42

Narrow Section to the Right of Main Path: From front row, front of cemetery

106. CHARLOTTE HANNAH SAMUELS, wife of Charles Samuels, died 16 September 1933, aged 67

107. CHARLES SAMUELS, died 20 November 1944, aged 82

108. ISIDORE SAMUELS, 12 October 1941, aged 51, husband of Maie and father of Jane and Susan

109. JULIUS SAMUELS, died 27 September 1947, aged 59, husband of Josephine and father of Barbara and Pamela. Also in memory of Josephine Irene (née Woolf), wife of Julius (1896-1977)

110. CONRAD SAMUELS, died 25 May 1952, aged 73

111. EDGAR SMAUELS, died 23 May 1958, husband of Joy and father of Felicity and Amanda

Post-1940 Section

ROW 1

112. ASSER OSCAR HEINEMANN, died April 1941, aged 63

113. ANNIE FINEGOLD, widow of Joseph Finegold, died 31 January 1941, aged 72

114. LISI FRIEDLANDER, died 16 December 1940

115. ANNIE SOLOMON, died 3 May 1941

ROW 2

116. YETTA KAPELMAN, died 19 September 1941, aged 47

117. VIKTOR GROSS, died 19 June 1942, aged 62

118. Gap

119. PILOT OFFICER H D ABRAMS, Air Observer, Royal Canadian Air Force, died 3 August 1941 aged 24

ROW 3

120. RACHEL CAPLIN, wife of Aaron Caplin of Leytonstone, London

121. RACHEL GOODING, died at Exeter, 5 February 1945, aged 70

122. SSAMUEL EIDLESTEIN, died 29 January 1945, aged 75

123. BRONCHE BAS TUVYEH, MRS B KENNEDY, 16 November 1944

Large gap

124. MAJOR GORDON CECIL KENNARD, MC, born 20 June 1884, died 7 December 1943

125. ADA STOLOFF, wife of Rev. W Stoloff, died 3 March 1945

ROW 4

Large gap before tombstones begin

126. MIRIAM HARRIS, died 4 March 1950, aged 83; and Isidore Abraham Harris, died 20 March 1950, aged 81

127. AGNES MARTHA LEVINE, died 10 November 1948, aged 47, wife of Israel Levine

128. MILLICENT HOLLANDER, wife of Abe Hollander, died 9 June 1945; and of Abe Hollander, died 15 May 1962

129. ELIZABETH BARNARD, died 6 June 1945 aged 84

130. ANDRE BLOK, died 16 June 1941, aged 71, husband of Clara. Headstone on left hand side of path, parallel to Hetty Wilhelm

ROW 5

131. HARRIETTE COHEN, daughter of the late Rev Manasseh and Martha Cohen, died 14 January 1954, aged 85

132. J. LOEWY, 6 May 1901 – 27 February 1951, a loving husband and father

133. 1875-1953, in loving memory of my dearest auntie, original name illegible

Gap

134. JULIA BOAM, died 30 December 1951, aged 68

135. MORRIS ROSENBERG, died 28 November 1951, aged 75; and wife Eva Rosenberg who died 26 December 1968, aged 85

ROW 6

136. COLEMAN PHILIPSON, MA, LL.D. LITT.D. 1875-1958

137. WOOLF DANIELS, died 24 April 1956, aged 71

138. ISAAC JACK KURLANDER, died 25 March 1957, aged 69

139. ISAAC PHILIP HYAMS, son of Barnet Bairal, died 23 November 1956, aged 56

140. CHARLOTTE WEISE, 1905 - 1956

ROW 7

Large gap before tombstones begin

141. ELLIOT ALPERN, died 30 March 1961, aged 19

142. WILLIAM WOOLF BOAM, died 30 December 1963, aged 84

Gap

143. SAMUEL PALLEY, born 2 June 1896, died 12 November 1970

144. ROSE SABEL, died 22 September 1971, aged 71

ROW 8

145. LOUIS SABEL, died 19 July 1975, aged 77

146. HEYA GOLDA SCHWARTZ, died 31 March 1965, wife of Jacob Schwartz who died 2 June 1951

147. ISAAC GOLDMAN, 1871 - 1962

148. ELIZABETH LEVY, died 6 February 1976

149. HAROLD HARRIS, died 20 January 1980, aged 73

150. MATHILDA HYAMS, died 1979 (??)

151. MARGARET FINK, died 30 November 1979, school teacher

152. RICHARD ASHER ELLENBOGEN ELLIS, born 3 November 1915, died 18 September 1981, son of doctor Abraham Ellis and Rebecca Ellis

ROW 9 (by back wall)

153. MALCOLM ISBITT, died 12 July 1977, aged 37

154. JEANNIE CHARITON, died 2 March 1977, aged 83

Narrow Section to the Right of Main Path

(From back row towards the front)

155. DAVID STANLEY SEIGAL, 1924-1984

156. BERNARD ROSENBERG, died 26 January 1985, aged 74

157. MAURICE FREDERICK MITCHELL ALEXANDER, died 31 December 1987, aged 71, local reporter for the Express & Echo

158. GOLDA WEINBERG, died 2 August 1990

159. GOLDA ZULMAN, died 16 December 1990, aged 86

160. HETTY WILHELM (née Baron), died 5 May 1991

161. PHOEBE DAVIS, born 16 February 1901, died 23 February 1996

162. ABE SYDNEY QUAIT, born 5 May 1912, died 17 May 1993, husband of Margaret

163. BARBARA ALGAR, 19 August 1933 – 8 July 1997

164. DERRICK MICHAEL NAHUM, 24 December 1916 – 22 January 1998

165. BERTHA ROSE BOAM, 1930-2002

Large gap

166. THERESA SAMUELS, died 3 July 1976, aged 76

Along wall next to chapel, from left to right:

167. DERRICK DAVID BOAM, 1918-2007 and his beloved wife Ella (neé Levy), 1925-2011

168. ELLY POLLAK-WEIL, born 3 December 1913 Vienna, died 17 August 2005 Devon; also in memory of her parents Samuel Bock died 20 June 1942 Vienna and Hermine Bock, died 26 May Maly Trostinec

169. JOSEPHINE BEAVIS (née Boam), 1922-2008 and Leonard Beavis, 1920-2000

170. DEBORAH ADAMS, 1906-2002, beloved sister of the Boam family and cousin of Raymond and Lee Lyons

171. LILIAN RYAN, died 7 March 1998, sister of the Boam family

172. GERARD KLEIN, born 12 April 1923 Berlin, died 18 November 2003 Exeter

173. ISRAEL GERSHON HARRIS, 1881-1950, 'A man against men' (older tombstone)

174. RACHEL SHORTLAND 'RAE', 20 May 1916 – 5 June 1999 [middle of grass under a tree, near the chapel]

SECTION 2

NEW JEWISH CEMETERY

EXETER

In October 1985 the Exeter Hebrew Congregation held an open meeting to discuss the lack of space remaining in the cemetery in Magdalen Street. Exeter City Council was approached but as of the following year had been unable to find a new burial ground. In April 1986, at the direction of Frank Gent, discussions focused on reviving the *Chevera Kadisha* (burial society). The congregation eventually acquired a separate section in the Exwick Municipal Cemetery and the first burial there took place in January 1992.

JS 0001	ROSEMARY DEBORAH JOSEPH, 11 January 1927 – 21 January 1992, aged 65, resident of Shillingford St George, Exeter
JS 0002	DAEL EUGENE SMITH, date of burial 19 February 1992, aged 42, of Plymouth, no headstone
JS 0003	ELIZABETH LOEWY, aka Ella or Elizabeth Conway, 1908-1994, aged 86, buried 20 June 1994, resident of Exeter
JS 0004	ANNIE ROSE FERN, 1921-1995, wife of the late Alfred Fern, aged 74, buried 6 April 1995, resident of Torquay

JS 0005	RUTH MARJORIE JOSEPH, 30 Sept 1923 – 25 July 1996, died Neumarkt, Germany, aged 72, resident of Shillingford St George, Exeter
JS 0006	MICHAEL LEIGH ALGAR, buried 4 October 1999, aged 63, resident of Holcombe near Bath, no headstone
JS 0007	BARBARA LARAH, 1956 – 2001, daughter of Esther and Monty Larah of Manchester, died Barnstaple aged 44, resident of Bickington, Barnstaple
JS 0008	CYRIL PENEL (Betzalel ben Shabsai Lev), 1924 – 2007, died 27 April 2007 aged 83, resident of Budleigh Salterton
JS 0009	MARJEM CHATTERTON, died 28 January 2010 aged 93, resident of Exeter, no headstone
JS 0010	Empty
JS 0011	TAMARA GRIFFITH, née Loberman, 23 Oct 1924 – 4 March 2002, died aged 77, resident of Horsham, West Sussex
	Also: DAVID HENRY GRIFFITHS, 15 June 1953 – 18 April 2005, aged 51, beloved son of William and Tamara, husband of Morag; resident of Topsham, Exeter. Notes: ashes.
JS 0012	DAVID MARK FOOT, 16 March 1917 – 18 February 2009, aged 91, resident of Exeter. Notes: ashes
JS 0013	Empty
JS 0014	Empty

JS 0015   ISAAC BACHAR, died 2 December 2002 aged 65, resident of Exeter, wife of Isabella, children: Aliza, Rachel and Miriam

JS 0016   Reserved

JS 0017   Empty

JS 0018   ESTHER GRYNWALD, died 3 June 2008 aged 88, resident of Exeter, no headstone

SECTION 3

TORQUAY AND PAIGNTON JEWISH CEMETERY

The Torquay & Paignton Jewish burial ground lies in a designated section of the municipal cemetery in Colney End Road, Paignton. A survey of the site was first carried out by the author just prior to 2000 and every headstone photographed. This has proved to be an important record because today, although the earliest tombstones date back to only 1964, their inscriptions are now illegible. Others are found to be in a poor state.

Most of the headstones dating back to the 1980s, and in some cases the 1990s, are also now illegible. The wooden doors to the ohel (chapel) are in a sorry state, but it is still possible to read the plaque on it, which reads:

> This tablet was presented by the Torquay and Paignton Chevra Kadisha in memory of Sydney Solomon president for many years and an honorary life president in grateful recognition of devoted and valuable services rendered.

The burial ground is still in use even though the Torquay & Paignton Hebrew Congregation is defunct and its synagogue closed a few years ago. Torquay once had an active, thriving community during the Second World War with the arrival in the region of evacuees and refugees. It kept going for as long as possible, but the decision was taken a few years ago to close it. Surviving records are held in the Devon Record Office in Exeter.

A list of burials in the cemetery:

ROW 1

1. SIMON BENDER, 'though your smile is gone forever and your hand we cannot touch still we have so many memories of the one we loved so much. We miss you so. Wife Sheila, family and friends

2. FREDA BROWN (née Zakheim) who passed away 12 October 1996 aged 69 years

3. FRANK ARTHUR BERMAN, died 25 November 1992, aged 84

4. SADIE BERMAN, born 26 October 1904, died 25 May 1985, wife of Frank Arthur Berman

5. EZRA FREED, died 26 June 1983, aged 79

6. SAMUEL AARONS, died 31 October 1979

7. SONIA WHITE, 1903-1999, widow of Joseph, mother of Derek and Pam

ROW 2

1. HERMAN KAY, died 29 July 1976, aged 52

2. JOSEPH WHITE, 1893-1978, husband of Sonia

3. MOSES L ROBINSON, born 1912, died 1978

4. SYLVIA MAY ROBINSON, 1913-1992, wife of Moses

5. GLADYS BERMAN, died 27 May 1986, aged 79, wife of Jack Berman, mother of Enid and Cynthia

6. HARRY HART, died 30 March 1995, aged 75

ROW 3

1. DR JOSEPH LYONS, 1917-2010

2. ANNIE SALTER, 1913-2003, wife of Morris, a woman ahead of her time

Gap

3. MARK MONTY WAXMAN, 28 May 1985, aged 80

4. ALEXANDER DOKELMAN, died 27 April 1983, aged 64, husband of Nancy

5. ELSA WILZIG (Esther), 21 February 1893 – 25 April 1978

Gap

6. MARY BLACK, died 4 May 1978, aged 81, wife of Solomon, mother of David

7. ELIAS LEVINE, died 15 May 1972, aged 73

8. ANNIE BARNETT (née Silverman), mother of Joan, Lionel and Bernard, wife of SH Barnett, died 12 May 1964

9. MAJLOCK KRONENBERG, 23 October 1965

ROW 4

1. RACHEL BERTHA FREEDMAN, died 27 December 1971, aged 68

2. ISAAC (FRED) FREEDMAN, died 12 May 1967, aged 76

3. HENRY WILLINGER, died 9 August 1963, aged 70

4. FREIDA BUNT, died 30 March 1970

5. DOMAZ RODRECOUS DA COSTA (Taffy), died 20 September 1972, aged 55

Gap

6. HARRY SILVER, 1894-1978

7. RONALD MARKHAM, 31 July 1926 – 9 October 1982, husband of Ursula, father of Philip and David

8. RONALD LURIA, 30 March 1936 – 2 December 1984

9. AMY SARAH JACOBS, died 22 May 1995, aged 83

Gap

10. CAROLINE WHITE, 1929-2010

ROW 5

1. BOB WHITE, 1923 – 2004

Gap

2. MURIEL WHITE, 1932 – 1994

3 & 4. ANNE MURRAY, died 7 February 1984, aged 82, wife of David,

mother of Henry. Same grave: DAVID MURRAY, died 9 March 1986, aged 91 [double grave]

5. HENRY MAX GREEN, died 24 September 1981

Gap

6. DEBORAH BARNETT, died 15 October 1977, aged 77, mother of Sybil and Alan

7. AUGUSTA (CUSSIE) KOSKY, died 8 July 1970, mother of Tony and Philip

8. MAURICE KOSKY, died 8 December 1969, aged 63, husband of Cussie

9. HARRY HARRIS COLLINS (COVITZ), born 16 January 1915, died 20 September 1963

10. JACOB HENRY (JACK) MAZE, born 18 December 1909, died 15 October 1967, husband of Golda

ROW 6

1. ANTHONY HYMAN (TONY) KOSKY, 17 August 1932 – 27 October 2005, son of Gussie & Kay

2. GOLDA (GIRLIE) MAZE, born 25 December 1913, died 21 April 1978

3. JOSEPH FELDSTEIN, died 18 March 1964, aged 72, husband of Annie

4. ANNIE FELDSTEIN, died 8 October 1976, aged 81

5. JEAN JULIUS ALEXANDER BERNHARDT, born 1896, died 26 July 1972

Gap

6. RITA BROOKS, died 26 March 1978, aged 72

7. GERALD BURTON, died 3 May 1981, aged 66

8. HETTIE LYONS, died 19 May 1992 (??)

9. VERA LEES, died 20 November 1993, aged 86, wife of Maurice, mother of Avril and David

Gap

10. LEON FREDMAN, died 13 February 2000, aged 74

ROW 7

1. SYBIL BARNETT, died 12 June 1999 (28th Sivan 5759), aged 77

2. ALAN BARNETT, died 10 January 1992, aged 65 (5th Shevat 5752), son of the late Sidney and Debby Barnett

3. LEWIS SOLLEY, 1897 - 1982

4. SOPHIE SOLLEY, 1902 – 1981

5. FAY CHAPKIS, 4 March 1912 – 9 September 1981, 'a perceptive woman of great wit'

6. LEWIS CHAPKIS, 13 March 1894 – 14 August 1978, 'a brave man of much love'

7. BERNARD ELLISON, died 29 May 1972, aged 60

8. RUTH RACHELL WHYTE, died 6 December 19699.

9. MAURICE ZELIG GRUNBERG, born 8 December 1878, died 5

December 1964

10. ENID SYLVIA SINCLAIR, born 8 March 1930, died 24 April 1968, daughter of Gladys and Jack Berman

ROW 8

1. MAX PERETZ, died 21 November 1968, aged 66

2. ISAAC LEVY, died 15 September 1965

3. PEARL MELLOR, died 19 November 1969, aged 70

4. ABRAHAM MELLOR, died 25 April 1978, aged 79, father of Sonia, David and Michael

5. REVD. LOUIS WEIWOW, 1892 – 1976

6. MIRIAM WEIWOW, 1892 – 1979

Gap

7. BERNARD SOLLEY, 1925 – 1982

8. AUBREY DENNIS SOLLEY, died 7 February 1993, husband of Margaret Joan

At the Side of the Ohel

ROW 9

1. WALTER WYNATE, died 23 February 1990 (28th Shevat 5750), aged 87, husband of Marion

2. RUTH SUMMERFIELD, born 27 April 1909, died 4 January 2005

ROW 10

1. WOOLF LEPEK, died 3 January 1989 (26th Tevet 5749), aged 75

ROW 11

1. ALMA SNEDDON, 27 March 1905 – 23 September 1985

2. MAX KALI N (??), 1918-1987, barely legible

3. LAURA KING (née Lena Laura Warshauer), born 30 December 1922 Forst, Germany. Died 29 March 2004, Paignton

4. DARREN LEE JACOBSON, 1967 - 2007

Outside the Jewish cemetery in a section on its own are three tombstones with a Star of David and a cross on them (married out or converted?):

1. NORMAN COFFIN, died 26 May 1972, aged 53, husband of Valerie

2. WOOLF SCHAK, 15 August 1914 – 3 February 1972, husband of Rita

3. HARRY WILDER, died 20 March 1987, husband of Lily who joined him 18 December 1996

SECTION 4
OLD BURIAL GROUND
THE HOE, PLYMOUTH

The first Jewish burial in Plymouth took place circa 1748 in a private garden at Lambhay Green, by Plymouth Hoe. It was land owned or leased by Mrs Sarah Sherrenbeck, the widow of Joseph Jacob Sherrenbeck. This 'garden cemetery' was acquired by Plymouth Hebrew Congregation nearly fifteen years earlier than its purpose-built synagogue of 1762. As the community increased in size it became necessary to extend the small burial ground and thus in June 1758 another quarter acre of ground adjacent to the Sherrenbeck's property was purchased. It was extended further in 1811 under the names of three local Jewish men: Abraham Emanuel of Plymouth Dock (shopkeeper), Michael Nathan of Plymouth (shopkeeper) and Benjamin Levy (optician) of Plymouth, and a prominent non-Jew, John Saunders (gentleman) of Plymouth. Ultimately Mrs Sherrenbeck transferred the burial ground to the Plymouth Jewish community and this served the congregation unto the 1860s when a second plot at Gifford Place was acquired to meet the expanding needs of the community.

A large oval stone set into the wall commemorates the gift of £157 by Joseph Joseph to the Plymouth Congregation in 1796 to complete the purchase of the ground, although the inscription which was recorded in the 1960s is now completely illegible. An ohel once stood in the cemetery but has since vanished. It was used not only as a place to perform the last rites of washing the body, but also as a shelter for the members of the Congregation who took it in turn to guard a newly interred body to prevent it being 'snatched'.

Revd Dr M. Berlin originally made a transcript of ninety-five inscriptions of headstones, by no means all of those which were then extant. However of the ninety-five inscriptions which he noted down, forty-five have totally disappeared, i.e nearly half in a comparatively short space of 70 years. After a careful study of the surviving tombstones, the late Rabbi Dr Bernard Susser deciphered a total of a hundred and forty-six inscriptions. Today it is not possible to fully read them. Inscriptions originally were mostly in Hebrew, and occasionally the English name on the reverse. Susser noted mistakes due to masons who were ignorant of Hebrew. At first only Hebrew was used on the stones. From around 1825 English began to appear on the reverse side of stones in Plymouth. English appeared on the same side as the Hebrew on headstones from about 1840.

Under some inscriptions listed below are extra biographical information in italics. The original sections identified and noted down by Rev Dr Berlin and then Rabbi Dr Susser are followed here.

SECTION A

A1. Reichla bat Menahem, wife of the late Gabbai Zedakah Mordecai died 23 Av 5566 [= 7 August 1806]

A2. Broken and illegible

A4. Broken and illegible

A5. The worthy Isaac Eisak ben Jacob from Totnes, died 15 Kislev [= 24 November 1809] aged 73. *Isaac Jacobs, silversmith, who married Betsy Levy of Barnstaple*

A6. Missing or illegible

A12. Missing or illegible

A13. Here is buried his honour Judah ben his honour Joseph, a prince and honoured amongst philanthropists, who executed good deeds, died in his house in the City of Bath, Tuesday, and was buried here on Sunday, 19 Sivan in the year 5585 [= 5 June 1825]. In memory of Lyon Joseph Esq (merchant of Falmouth, Cornwall) who died at Bath June AM 5585/VE 1825. Beloved and respected.

Lyon Joseph (1744 1825) made a fortune shipping goods to the ports of the peninsula unoccupied by Napoleon.

A14. See Berlin 13/10, below.

A15. A perfect man and upright, a God fearing man, Menasseh ben Zvi. He was buried and died on Friday 16 Heshvan 5589 [= 24 October 1828]. *Emanuel Hart from Biala, watchmaker and silversmith in Southside Street, Plymouth and later premises in Clements Lane, Plymouth*

A16. Illegible

A17. Illegible

A18. Here lies a faithful man the Parnas and Manhig Alexander ben Samuel. Died and buried Thursday 10 Av 5593 [= 1 August 1832]. *Alexander Samuel who lived in Truro circa 1815.*

A19. Abraham ben Aaron, buried 11 Shevat 5593 [= 31 January 1833]. *Abraham Aaron married Phoebe, daughter of Abraham Joseph. They had eight children.*

A20. [In a semi circle at the top] 'Thou didst make his name Abraham, and Thou didst find his heart perfect before Thee' [Neh. 9;7]. Here dwells a faithful man, fearful of sin [4 lines of poetry follow]. The Parnas and Manhig, his name well known, Abraham ben Issachar Jacob. Died on Monday 17 Iyar and buried on the 18th in the year 'in order that you may be righteous'. May he rest and rise for his lot with all who are buried here. [Reverse] To the memory of Abraham Levi died 25 May 5594 [= 1834] aged 55 years. *Abraham Levy. He married Zipporah bat Aaron Moses ben Abraham, c.1810.*

A21. A God fearing man, the Parnas and Manhig Eliezer ben Solomon zts"l, died Wednesday 25 Heshvan and buried Thursday after it, 5596 [= 18 November 1835]. He lies here but shall arise at the end of days.

Lazarus Solomon from Lublin, a scholar, referred to as Torani, in Plymouth before 1802. He married Esther bat Abraham, who died 1831 and then Mathilda.

A22. Aryeh Judah ben Zvi. [Reverse] Lyon Levi departed this life 11 August 5596 [= 1836].

Son-in-law of Judah Moses. Plymouth Dock merchant, bankrupt April 1811.

A23. Isaac ben Avigdor he lived 41 years, died Friday 26 Av 5598 [= 17 August 1838].
[Reverse] To the memory of Solomon Lyon. [It had a long and barely legible piece of poetry]. *A pen and quill manufacturer in Plymouth before 1822, then goldsmith.*

A24. Illegible.

A25. [Reverse] Henry Phillips, aged 6 years, son of Charles and Anne Phillips. *Also near this spot lie Flora and Rachel their infant children.*

A26. My only son Isaac whom I loved, the son of Meir, Cantor here, 56. *Isaac, the son of Revd Meyer Stadthagen.*

A27. .... in his house in the city of ... Tuesday 14 Sivan and buried here on Sunday 19 Sivan 5585 [= 1825].

A28. A child of delights Avigdor ben Samuel died Adar Rishon 5562 [= February 1802]. *Avigdor Hart aged 5.*

A29. Missing.

A30. The bachelor Abraham ben ?

A31. Missing or illegible

A42. Missing or illegible

A43. Joel ben Issachar Jacob, died on Sabbath, 22 Shevat 5591 [= 5 February 1831] and his soul shall dwell with the righteous who dwell here until He maketh death to vanish in life eternal. [Reverse] Joel Levy beloved husband of Rachel Levy, aged ?55 years.

Joel Levy, a member of the Plymouth Meshivat Nefesh Society in 1795. Insured as a silversmith in Market Street, Plymouth, in 1800. He was a Navy Agent near The Parade, Plymouth in 1816, and was a silversmith in Market Street in 1822. His wife Rachel bat Joseph died 14 February 1822.

A44. See Berlin O8, below.

A45. Friedcha bat P"M Abraham Isaac, wife of Abraham ben Aaron, buried Sunday, 11 Heshvan 5593 [= 4 November 1832]. *She was Phoebe, daughter of Abraham Joseph I and wife of Abraham Aaron.*

A46. Miss Bila bat Solomon aged 51 years, died Monday 18 Kislev 5594 [= 30 November 1833]. [Reverse] Bile Nathan.

A47. Esther, wife of Mordecai ben Samuel SGL. [Reverse] Esther Mordecai died 19 August 5593 [= 1834].

A48. Tella wife of Jonah from the State of Silesia who died with a hoary head aged 72, on 12 Nisan 5594 [= 21 April 1834]. *Revd Dr Berlin read, 'Gella died 12th Nisan 5595 [= 11 April 1835]*

A49. Breincha bat Abraham, wife of Samuel ben Hayim. [Reverse] Elizabeth Hyman died 19 Kislev 5596 [= 10 December 1835] aged 52 years.

A50. Betsy Jacobs, wife of Isaac Jacobs of Totnes... 5596 [= 1836]. *Betsy Jacobs (1759 1836) née Levy of Barnstaple and married Isaac Jacobs of Totnes in 1784.*

A51. Samuel ben Hayim. [Reverse] Samuel Hyman, died 23 November 5599 [= 1838] aged 73 years. *Samuel Hyman (1771 1838), born Bohemia, came to England via Dover 1788. Married Betsy daughter of Abraham Moses, and had 11 children.*

A52. Missing or illegible

A55. Missing or illegible

A56. Here lies the modest and worthy woman Reichla bat Abraham, wife of the late Naphtali Benjamin. She died on Friday 26 Adar 5577 [= 14 March 1817] with a good name. A woman who fears the Lord, she shall be praised. She went to her rest 17 years after her husband, and there they shall rest in honour with all the righteous men and righteous women in the Garden of Eden, and they shall rise at their portion at the end of days.

Wife of Naphtali Benjamin and one of the respected women of the community. Her husband was a box maker, born in 1725 at Ilbersheim near Mannheim. The headstone has been removed from its place and lies next to B126.

A57. Missing or illegible

A59. Missing or illegible

A60. Hannah bat David KZ, wife of Issachar Ber, Santapel, SGL. Died Monday ?25 Adar 5581 [= March 1821].

A61. Missing

A62. Reichle bat Joseph wife of the late Joel Levy, died 23 Shevat 5582 [= 14 February 1822]. *Rachel Levy*

A63. Missing

A66. Missing

A67. The scholar Matathias ben Rabbi Shabbetai the Priest, from Poland, died 9 Av 5573 [= 5 August 1813] at half his days. *Mattis Cohen.*

A68. 17 Elul 5593 [= 1 September 1833].

A69. Moses ben Aryeh Lobell from the State of Germany who pitched his tent in the City of Birmingham, and who conducted there the needs of the Congregation. He was buried 5 Av 5594 [= Sunday, 10 August 1834]. Moses Lobell of Birmingham, died 5594 aged 64 years.

A70. Missing.

A71. Gabriel ben Judah died 28 Iyar 5598. [Reverse] Gabriel Rosenthal died 27 May [= 1835] aged 33 (?55) years.

Came from Poland, a son was born posthumously to him in July 1835 and given his name Gabriel. His widow Ann married in 1844 Mark Levy of Guernsey.

A72. An old man Avigdor ben Moses Isaac, died with hoary head ... [Reverse] Francis Lyon died 23 Shevat 5597 [= 28 January 1837] aged 85 years. *Francis Lyons, watchmaker in Pike Street 1822. His children were Solomon, Judah and Mathilda.*

A73. Here lies Martha bat the Haver Judah the cantor, wife of Abraham Emdon, who died on Thursday 15 Iyar, and was buried on Thursday 18 Iyar 5598 [= 10 May 1838].

A74. Here lies the body of Elizabeth Abrahams who died Friday night and was buried on Sunday 22 Adar Sheni 5590, aged 42 years. May her soul rest in peace.

A75. Missing.

A76. The bachelor ?Zvi ?Hirsh ben Asher died Tamuz 55(?70) [= July ?1810] or 55(?90) [= July ?1830].

A77. Missing or illegible

A82. Missing or illegible

A83. A broken slate stone, only the name barely legible. See Berlin Q19, below.

A84. Missing

A85. In 1963 barely legible by Susser. See Berlin Q16 below.

A86. Missing

A91. Missing

A92. Moses ben Jacob from the City of London which was the city of his birth died Thursday night and buried Friday 3 Elul 5598 [= 24 August 1838]. [Reverse] Moses Solomon formerly of Scotland .... London.

A93. Judah ben Isaac, died Sunday and buried Tuesday 8 Sivan 5540 [= 9 June 1840]. [Reverse] Levin Jacobs aged 49 years.

A94. [Reverse] Betsy ... Jacobs, (?) daughter of the late Lewis Jacobs.

A95. Missing or illegible

A99. Missing or illegible

A100. Merela [Berlin reads Merka] bat Joseph, wife of Judah Zvi ben Solomon died and buried 5 Elul 5572 [= 16 August 1812].

A101. Missing or illegible

A103. Missing or illegible

A104. David ben Solomon. *David son of the late Revd Solomon Lyons, formerly of Cambridge, who died at Brixham on his voyage to Naples, 8 February 1819 aged 20 years.*

A105. Missing or illegible

A108. Missing or illegible

A109. 5525 [= 1835]

A122. Missing or illegible

A124. Missing or illegible

A125. An upright and honoured man, the elderly bachelor, one hundred years old at his death, ... Isaac ben Rabbi Joseph, died on the Holy Sabbath the 11th of [month omitted on stone] and was buried on the 12th of [month omitted on stone] 5574 [= 1813/1814] with a good name.

A126. Ze'ev Wolf ben Naphtali, died and buried 13 Tishri 5574 [= 7 October 1813].

A127. Joseph ... died Sunday 27 Sivan 5582 [= 16 June 1822].

A128. Missing

A129. Missing

A130. An upright and faithful man ... ben Naphtali. Died 5559 [= 1799].

A131. Illegible

A132. Illegible

A133. Samuel ben Judah, died 1 Adar Sheni 5627. [Reverse] Samuel Ralph died 17 March 1867 aged 64 years.

Samuel Ralph was a grandson of Abraham Ralph of Barnstaple who died December 1805 and who had been established there since 1765 holding services in his house. His father Judah or Lewis Ralph was a Navy Agent in Plymouth in 1812 and was secretary to a Masonic Lodge. Samuel was born 18 June 1803 and circumcised by Joseph Joseph.

SECTION B

B1. Here lies Avigdor ben Judah who died the eve of Tuesday 10 Heshvan and was buried on Wednesday its morrow in the year 5610. In memory of Frederik Ralph, who departed this life 15 October 5611 [= 1850], aged ?46 years. *A marine store dealer on Southside Quay in 1844. He was a brother of Samuel Ralph.*

B2. Here lies the wise bachelor Abraham ben Baruch SGL, died Friday 26 Shevat and was buried Sunday, 28 Shevat 5548 [= 4 February 1788 but the day and date do not coincide]. May he remain in his grave and rise in his turn at the end of days. *A member of the Plymouth Congregation before 1759. He is described on his tombstone as HaBachur HaYashish = The Wise Bachelor.*

B3. This man, perfect and upright in his works/ Whose deeds were righteous/ His death bemoaned by his friends and aquaintances/ At fifty eight years of age he was gathered to his people [Ze'ev] ben Solomon. In the year HaBrith, according to the major order of counting [= 5612]. W. Solomon, died ?2 ?March 5612 [= 1852].

B4. Our lives are in Thy hands O God, and our days are as nought before Thee. Here lies David ben Abraham for 50 years a member of the congregation of this town, died and buried with a good name on Friday ?27 Tamuz 5600 [= 28 July 1840] aged 76 years.

David Abraham, silversmith, born 1762, came to England via Dover in 1789. He married Rose, daughter of Isaac and Betsy Jacobs of Totnes.

B5. Illegible

B6. Jacob ben Judah, died ? Thursday ?8 Sivan ?5553 [= May 1793] or possibly ?5653 [= May 1893]

B7. B8. Illegible double stone.

B9. Eliezer ben Abraham Emden died on 16 Shevat and buried on 17 Shevat 5604 [= 6 February 1844]. The days of his years which he lived were eighty three.

Eliezer Emden born 1764 Amsterdam, came to England 1786, remained in London until 1794, then to Portsmouth until 1798, moved to Plymouth in 1798 and died there. A dealer in old clothes who achieved some financial stability as a pawnbroker in Cornwall Street, Devonport in 1844.

B10. The Parnas and Manhig Samuel ben Solomon Phineas, died Tuesday 17 Tamuz and buried Wednesday in the year 5605 [= 22 July 1845].

Samuel Levy (1811 1845) whose wife was Phoebe. He had a Fancy Warehouse at 35 Bedford Street. His father was Phineas Levy of Devonport, one of the first Jews to hold elected civic office in England.

B11. Here lies the aged, full of years, Alexander ben Abraham who died Nisan 5610 [= March 1850]. *Sender Alexander, the tombstone inscription is worn and probably incorrectly read. He was born in Devon, a tailor in Cambridge Street in 1841, Parnas of the Congregation in 1815 and 1816.*

B12. Sacred to the memory of Mark Mordecai, who departed this life 2 May 5609 [= 1849] in his 70th year. *Mordecai ben Samuel whose wife Esther died 10 August 1833. Sons were Samuel, Jacob, Zvi, Simha, and daughter Anna married Isaac Stone. He was a brother in law of Phineas Levy.*

B13. Judah, thy brothers bless thee [Gen. 49:8]/ Your name is praised as generous hearted/ The poor and orphans ... at thy table/ With a perfect heart thou didst serve the Lord thy God/ In the bond of life shall thy soul rest/ Judah ben Moses, died 20 Av 5609. Lyon Lazarus died 8 August 5609 [= 1849] aged 59 years.

Lyon or Lippa Lazarus, married Mathilda who was born in Bideford in 1801. He was an optician in Frankfort Street in 1836. Three of his children Abraham, Daniel and Solomon died in 1832, 1833 and 1836. He probably came from Exeter. Surviving children in 1851 were Mosely (general dealer), Fanny (dressmaker) who married Nathan Lazarus in 1853, Frank (merchant apprentice), Hezekiah (scholar) with a niece Hannah Lyons (dressmaker) and Juliana Marks of Portsmouth.

B14. The bachelor Hayim ben ... Hyman Solomon died ? August 5609 [= 1849]. *Hyman Solomon = Hayim ben Isaiah (1838 1849) son of Josiah and Rosa Solomon.*

B15. Nathan ben Joseph KZ, died Friday ?26 Tishri and was buried on the Monday after it, 5610 [= 12th October 1851].

Nathan Joseph alias Altmann, born 1766 Ransporke, Bohemia, landed Gravesend 1784, in Dartmouth 1784, in Plymouth from 1802 in Broad Street (a jeweller). At 72 Fore Street, Plymouth Dock, Navy Agent in 1816. Property owner. He married Brina daughter of Abraham Joseph I. He left his property to his sons Sampson Altman and Michael Israel Altman both of Kingston, Jamaica, and both surgeons. Although in England for 65 years he signed his will in Hebrew characters.

B16. An elder, honoured amongst men, his heart did not hold back from bestowing loving kindness, Phineas ben Abraham Emdin, died with a good name Thursday 15 Av 5610 [= 24 July 1850].

Solomon (Selig) Emden. Born 1771 Amsterdam, and was in 9 Cat Street in 1803, and was a hatter. His wife was Freda bat Judah, died 1843 (B35). He was allowed to live in the Congregation's house next to the Synagogue.

B17. Hayim ben Mordecai. Hyman Levy died 14 Kislev 5611 [= 19 November 1850].

Hyman Levy came from Plock, Prussia, Poland.

B18. Jacob was a perfect man, upright in his flock/ He turned from wickedness, faithfulness was his love/ He departed from evil, his way was good/ The portion of Jacob is his inheritance/ A lion, with clean hands. J. P. Lyon died 23 Yiar [sic] 5612 [= 12 May 1852].

Judah P. Lyon (1794 1852) was born in Bideford, married Fanny (b. 1803, Swansea). Watchmaker and jeweller of 7 Union Street.

B19. Jacob ben Judah. John Levi died 10 Adar 5615 [= 28 February 1855].

John Levi (b. 1793, Portsmouth, general dealer. His wife was probably Elizabeth. His daughters: Eliza married Benjamin Jonas in 1841, Phoebe married Aaron Wolf in 1846, Julia married Edward Basch, Traphina married Sigmond Yager.

B20. A perfect and upright man, he walked in perfection and executed righteousness, a God fearing man all his days, Jacob ben the late Judah, he was 63 years old when he died on Tuesday 28 Nisan and was buried with a good name on Wednesday the 29th thereof in the year 5615. To the memory of Jacob Moses died 28 days in Nisan 5615 [= 16 April 1855] aged 63 years.

The Hebrew has three errors, possibly the fault of the mason. This Jacob Moses was probably the husband of Agnes, haberdasher, and father of Esther (milliner).

B21. By decree of the plague, Haya, wife of Jacob ben Ze'ev, died

47

Av 5592 [= August 1832].

Hannah Woolfson, wife of Jacob Woolfson of London who settled in Plymouth about 1819. She died in the cholera epidemic of 1832.

B22. Here lies an upright man amongst the princes. All his deeds was (sic) altruistic. And he clave to the living God. David ben Jacob from Bialin in Poland, died 12 Shevas (sic) 5565 [= 12 January 1805.]

David Jacob Coppel (b. 1748, Belleye (Biala) arrived via Gravesend in 1799. Resided in Comer Lane, Plymouth in 1803. He had a brother Menahem [= Emanuel Cohen].

B23. A God fearing man Ze'ev ben Judah from Shotwinitz in the State of Poland, died by decree of the plague on Thursday and was buried on 6 Av 5592 [= 2 August 1832.)

B24. Here is buried Aaron ben Yehiel who went the way of all the earth in the sixty eighth year of his life. Aaron Nathan died 21 February 5618 [= 1858] aged 69 years.

Aaron Nathan of 17 Pearl Street, Stonehouse in 1827, pitifully poor, became Constable for Stonehouse and in 1837 apprehended a gang of counterfeiters. A silver snuff box awarded to him for this exploit is now in the Jewish Museum, London. In 1851 he was superintendent of the Watch Force and lived at Fore Street, Stonehouse with his wife Mary and daughters Haranitha (dressmaker) and Sarah (milliner).

B25. Jacob [ben] Uri Shraga ben Moses, who lived eight and sixty years, died Thursday and buried Friday, 19 Shevat 5593 [= 7 February 1833]. Philip Moses. Near this spot lies the remains of Eleazer Moses.

B26. The bachelor, a Godfearing man, Jacob ben Uri Shraga, the priest from Lontschotz, died Av 5592 [= August 1832].

Jacob Philip Cohen, member of the Congregation in 1819.

He seems to be identical with Meyer Jacob Cohen, hardware dealer who died 16 August 1832. His will (DRO, Exeter, C794), made 15 August 1832 and signed with Hebrew characters, was sworn with effects under £100, the executor was Charles Marks.

B27. Gitla bat Zvi, who died in her old age on the Holy Sabbath Iyar 5613. In memory of Hannah Ralph who departed this life May 5613 [=1853] aged 87 years.

Hannah Ralph wife of Judah (Lewis) Ralph who was the son of Abraham Ralph I of Bideford. Their children were Samuel, 1803-67 (tomb A133); Frederick, 1804-1850 (tomb B1); Abraham, 1814-1890; Amelia, 1812-1874; and possibly George.

B28. [Reverse] Sydney Solomon.

B29. Solomon Samuel ben Solomon who went to Heaven aged 1 year and two months, on Friday 22 Adar 5629 [= 5 March 1869]. [Reverse] Charles Samuel Solomon.

B30. A child of delights ...

(Apparently a double stone.)

B31. Sarah bat Benjamin Aryeh. [Reverse] Sarah Levi died 2 February 5601 [= 1851] aged 78 years.

B32. Missing

B34. Missing.

B35. Here lies a woman who feared the Lord in her heart/ To help with loving kindness the living/ and the dead, Mrs/ Friedcha bat Judah, wife of Phineas ben Abraham Emden, died Monday 6 Adar Rishon 5603

[= 6 February 1843].

B36. [Reverse] Esther Simons.

B37. [Reverse] Rosie ... Sander Alexander, aged ?66 years.

B38. Yetta bat Mordecai the Levite, wife of Eliezer ben the late Abraham, died in her old age on the Holy Sabbath, 10 Tamuz 5606 [= 4 July 1846].

The wife of Eliezer Aaron, son of Abraham Aaron, who in turn was son in law of Abraham Joseph I.

B39. [Reverse] [?] Harris.

B40. Esther bat ?Judah, wife of Alexander.

B41. Rachel Yettela bat Abraham, wife of Avigdor Isaac, died Nisan 5609 [= March 1849].

Sara Lyon.

B41a. Abraham ben ... died and buried 22 Adar 5566 [= 12 March 1806]. *Abraham Daniel, miniaturist and painter, died in Plymouth and left £20 to the synagogue.*

B42. Here lies the aged woman/ Who kept the commandments of the Lord/ And was gathered up in good hoary age/ Mrs Miriam bat Abraham Zvi KZ. Died 4 Iyar 5609. Meriam Abrahams died 25 April 5609 [= 1849] aged 96 years.

B42a. The child of delights Jacob ben Elijah Moss, born on Friday, 12th Tishri 5573 [= 18 September 1812], died and buried Friday 4 Nisan 5575 [= 14 April 1815].

His father was Elias Moss of George Street, Plymouth Dock. Navy Agent in 1816. Elias was brother to Barrow Moss.

B43. 5577 [=1817].

B43a. Sacred to the memory of Mordecai Levi son of Lyon and Leah Levi, died 3 Av 5577 [= 16 July 1817] aged 5 years and 2 months.

B44. Blima bat Eliezer wife of Isaac from Portsmouth. [Reverse] Blumey, wife of Isaac Marks of Portsmouth died December 5610 [= 1849] aged 77 years.

B45. Leah bat Issachar Baer, wife of Zvi ben Judah.

Wife of Zvi ben Judah Lyons from Warsaw, who in 1810 is described in Congregational records as a fringe maker. They lived in Devonport.

B46. Miss Pessla bat Simeon the Levite, died Tuesday ?25 Tevet 5610 [= ?9 January 1850]. [Reverse] In memory of Eliza Levi ....

B46a. Joseph ben Isaac, died first day of Rosh Hodesh Shevat 5591 [= 15 January 1831].

Joseph Isaac of Devonport.

B47. Telza wife of Abraham Joseph. [Reverse] Eliza Joseph, died 4 Shevat 5610 [= 17 January 1850], aged 42 years.

She was the daughter of Lemon Wolf, granddaughter of Moses Jacob of Redruth, and great granddaughter of Zender Falmouth. Her husband was Abraham Joseph II, and her children include Solomon, Hannah and Eliza.

B48. Miriam bat Abraham wife of Nathan from Dartmouth. [Reverse] Miriam Jacobs, wife of Nathan Jacobs, formerly of Dartmouth, 5610 [= 1850].

Miriam Jacobs was born in Devon in 1771; she was a silversmith in 1841 in Bedford Street, Plymouth. Her sons were Alexander, Jacob and Angel; her daughters: Betsy married B. L. Joseph of Liverpool; Martha (predeceased her mother) married Isaac Emanuel of Southampton; Zipporah married Hyman Hyman of Plymouth. Her nephews are said to have founded Crockfords.

B49. Ginandel bat Judah, wife of Judah, 5611 [= 1851].

Nandell Moses, probably the wife of Judah Moses I. She was born in Devon in 1766, and in 1841 was an 85 year old shopkeeper in the High Street, Plymouth.

B50. [Reverse] Leah (?) Levi.

(Front: Illegible)

B51. Hannah bat Isaac, wife of Judah, died on the Holy Sabbath, ?20 Tevet 5612 [= 12 January 1852]. [Reverse] Ann wife of Mark Levy aged ?43 years.

Ann, widow of Gabriel Rosenthal who died 27 May 1835, daughter of Isaac Mark. She married Mark Levy II in 1844. He was in business at Cornet Street, Guernsey and died there on 23 December 1848.

B52. Rachel bat Abraham, wife of Aaron. Rachel Bellem.

Rachel Bellam or Bellem (b. 1783, Plymouth), died 1863. Her husband was Aaron Bellam of Dartmouth, where her three children Harriet, a deaf and dumb seamstress, Jacob, general dealer, and Abraham, a dyer were born.

B53. Illegible.

B53a. Aaron ben Mordecai, died Monday 11 Av 5555 [= 27 July 1795].

He was born 26 March 1786 and was the fifth child to be circumcised by Joseph Joseph.

B54. Missing.

B55. Frumat bat Moses, wife of Abraham.

She was the first wife of Abraham Emden, she died 13 May 1838.

B56. A child's stone, illegible.

B57. [Reverse] Kitty, wife of Phinehas Levi, also her daughter Traphina.

Kitty Levi born Portsea 1788, died after 1851. Her husband was a Navy Agent of 15 Catherine Street, Devonport, and was one of the first Jews elected to Civic office in England.

B58. Leah bat Mordecai, wife of Abraham Emdin, died Av 5611 [= August 1851]. [Reverse] Leah wife of Abraham Emdon.

Lydia Emden (b. Devonport 1811), daughter of Mordecai Davis of Market Street, Plymouth, second wife of Abraham Emden. Her children were Clarence, Eleazar, Clare Solomon, Mark.

B58a. Zvi ben Moses, died Sunday and buried Monday 9 Iyar 5536 [= May 1776].

B59. [Reverse] Rebecca .... Lemon Wolf. W*ife of Lemon Wolf (the son of Hyman Woolf of Penzance). Rebecca was a daughter of Moses Jacob and Sarah Moses, and a granddaughter of Zender of Falmouth*

B60. [Reverse] Rosetta Solomon ?wife of Isaac Solomon. *She was Rosa bat Asher ben Hayim, a daughter of Hyman Woolf of Penzance. She was born in Cornwall, circa 1810/1811. Her children were Solomon, Sarah, Henry, Julia, Ellen E, Simon W, David. Her husband had a fancy goods warehouse at 22 Whimple Street, Plymouth. Rosetta's older sister Eliza was the first wife of Abraham Joseph II.*

B61. Fanny, beloved wife of Joseph Joseph, died ?Av ?5615.

Fanny Joseph was born in Poland 1815, daughter of Lazarus Solomon of Plymouth. She married Joseph Joseph of Redruth who moved to Plymouth in 1849 to 29 Whimple Street as a silversmith and mineralogist. Their children were Solomon, Phoebe, Henry, Esther, Sarah, Gertrude, Rose, Julia, Florence.

B62. Miriam bat Moses, wife of Aaron Nathan. May her pains and affliction which she bore in her life be an atonement for her sins. Died Friday

5 Heshvan 5618. Mary Nathan died 23 October 5618 [= 1858] aged 61 years.

B63. Miss Sarah bat Aaron, aged 38 years, died Tuesday Rosh Hodesh Kislev 5632. [Reverse] In loving memory of Sarah, daughter of Aaron and Mary Nathan, died 14 November 1871, aged 38.

B64. Bila bat Eliakim, died ?2 Kislev 5619 [= December 1859]. [Reverse] Elizabeth ... John Levi.

B65. Sarah bat Mordecai to the grief of her parents. [Reverse] Sarah Levy died 2 Tevet 5619 [= 9 December 1858], aged 15 years.

B66. Miss Gitla bat Isaac, died 5619 [= 1859]. [Reverse] Julia Marks, sister of Charles Marks.

Julia Marks was a strawbonnet maker in Cornwall Street in 1836.

B66a. The bachelor Moses ?Menahem ben Solomon, died [?] Heshvan ?5564 [= October ?1804].

B67. Bila bat Moses Isaac. She was 60 years old at her death. [Reverse] Arabella, wife of Myer Stadthagen, died 26 Nisan 5622 [= 26 April 1862] aged 61 years. *Daughter of Judith Jacob and Moses Isaac Joseph of Redruth, granddaughter of Zender of Falmouth.*

B68. The Parnas and Manhig to his congregation, Abraham ben Joseph. [Reverse] Abraham Joseph died 28 Eyar 5628 [= 20 May 1868]. *Abraham Joseph II (1799-1868), born Plymouth, married first on 31 January 1828 Eliza Wolf, daughter of Asher Wolf (1811 1850) of Penzance. Second wife was Rose who died 1896. By his first wife he had Rose, Hyman, Henry, Moses, Solomon, Sarah, David, Ruth, Hannah and Eliza. By his second wife he had Floretta. A bill broker in 1851 of 6 Mulgrave Place, Plymouth, Slop man to Prince William Henry. Friend of Chief Rabbi Nathan Adler, to whom he bequeathed his library.*

B69. A woman of valour and of upright heart, Sheincha, wife of cantor Lima [?Lita], died Wednesday, the eve of Rosh Hodesh Nisan 5553 [= 13th March 1793]. *The first reference to Cantor Lima is in 1796 when he was appointed Reader at £25 per annum. His salary went up to £42 per annum in 1802 and £50 per annum in 1816.*

B70. Mordecai ben Israel, an old man and honoured, who served in the fear of the Lord. Died with hoary head on Tuesday, 14 Shevat and buried on Wednesday in the year ?5618 [?= Friday 29 January 1858].

B71. Samuel ben Menahem the Priest, an honourable and faithful man from the stock of martyrs, eager to do loving kindness to the poor and hastening to his prayers, evening, morning and noon. Died 5 Iyar 5620 [= 27 April 1860]. *Samuel Cohen, referred to in Congregational records of 1820 as 'from Chelmsford', and seems to have travelled through Plymouth frequently about 1821. In 1846 it seems as though he was in some financial* *but he left £5 to the Synagogue when he died in 1860.*

B72. [Reverse] Marcus Wolf.

Ze'ev ben Mordecai (b.1781- died c.1860). Born Poland, married to Kitty also from Poland, left £1 to Synagogue at his death.

B73. Aaron.

B74. Judah Lyon. *Judah ben Avigdor. Probably son of Francis Lyons, died 1837. Brother of Solomon Lyons and Mathilda Lazarus. Watchmaker in Bedford Street, Plymouth 1836.*

B75. Illegible, but a ewer and basin at the head of the stone.

B76. Here lies a man who walked in uprightness and righteousness, he feared the Lord God all the days of his life. 32 years he was cantor here in the Holy Congregation of Plymouth. Meir ben Rabbi Isaac, he died on Monday, the 7th day of Passover, aged 58 years and was buried with great honour on the last day of the Passover, 5622. Myer Stadthagen died 21 Nisan 5622 [= 21 April 1862] aged 58. *Myer Stadthagen, born Prussia 1804, married Arabella. Their children were Selina, Phoebe, Sarah, Ellen and Isaac.*

B77. Abraham ben Yekutiel. ... buried with honour ... [Reverse] Abraham Kaufman, died 16 January 1863, aged 54 years. May his soul rest in peace. *Abraham Kaufman, hawker, born Prussia, bachelor. Described as a watchmaker when administration of his effects is granted to his brother Bernard Kaufman.*

B78. Miss Harriet Nathan.

Miss Harriet Nathan born Plymouth 1773, an aunt of Abraham Ralph II, probably the sister of Hannah Ralph. Listed in the Plymouth Directory, 1850 under 'gentry' and of Bedford Street.

B78a. Joseph ben Judah Jacob.

Joseph Jacob Sherrenbeck who came from Sherrenbeck in Germany and was the leader of the Plymouth Congregation in 1745. Is first heard of in 1734 at the Assizes at Taunton when he was found guilty of criminal conversation with the wife of Lazarus Chadwick, for which he was fined £20 and imprisoned for 2 years. He was a prominent business man. He and his wife were generous benefactors to the synagogue. He died between 1779 and 1782.

B79. Miss Rachel ben Jacob Judah, died 22 Tamuz 5629 [= 1 July 1869]. Reverse: R. Benjamin aged 88 years.

Rachel Benjamin, born Plymouth, feather maker, daughter of Levi Benjamin (cantor in Plymouth in 1813). She lived at 43 Claremont Street in 1851. She and a Miss E. Benjamin gave £7. 5s. to the Appeal for the Gifford Place Cemetery in 1858.

B80. Hannah bat Menahem the Levite, died Adar Sheni ?5635 [? = March 1875].
Hannah Jonas.

B81. Illegible.

B81a. Shraga ben Abraham KZ, died 13 Shevat 5551 [= 17 January 1791].

Hands of priest on the stone.

B82. Leah bat Shemaiah, wife of Menahem ben Jacob the priest, aged 81 years.

Her husband was Emanuel Cohen (born in Carlsberg, near Mannheim 1775), came to England via Gravesend in 1801, stayed in London for a short time and came to Plymouth in 1802. He left Plymouth in 1820 for Falmouth and Redruth.

B83. An upright and pure man, the late Gershon ben Judah Jacob, died Kislev 5542 [= December 1781].

Gershon Sherrenbeck, brother of Joseph Jacob Sherrenbeck.

B84. The woman elder Mrs ... wife of .... died Tishri 5543 [= September 1783].

B85. Illegible.

B86. Jacob Zvi ben Joseph. Reverse: Jacob Lyons.

Jacob Lyons (b. 1795, Poland) of 19 Barrack Street, East Stonehouse, general dealer in 1851. Children were: Rosa, Rebecca, Moses, Isaac, Amelia and Aaron. Rosa married George Norman, a secretary of the Synagogue in 1861.

B87. Here lies a man who feared God, his body lies in the ground, but his soul is in the Garden of Eden. Ze'ev Hayim ben Eleazer who lived 58 years and died with a good name on Friday the 8th of Adar Sheni and was buried with great honour on the 11th thereof in the year 5627. In memory of Woolf Emden died 15 March 1867, aged 58 years.

Woolf Emden (b. 21 April 1810), the son of Eliezer Emden. In 1851 he was a draper of 19, High Street. He married Rebecca Franco, daughter of John Franco.

B88. Jacob Joseph ben Aryeh, died 21 Kislev 5624 [= 2 December 1863]. Aged 58 years. Reverse: Jacob Joseph.

Susser's note: On an 1858 inscription in the Plymouth synagogue his Hebrew name is Isaac Joseph ben Aryeh.

B89. Abraham ben Aaron Bellem, the reaper passed over him and he died 27 Tishri 5627. Abraham Bellem died 6 October 5627 [= 1866] aged 44 years.

His father was Aaron ben Hayim of Dartmouth.

B90. Here lies the worthy bachelor it is a duty to remember him in honour/ because he dealt in faithfulness,/ charity to the poor he gave,/ his righteousness will remain forever,/ may he reap the reward of the righteous./ He left his wealth as an everlasting memorial/ to see the pleasantness of the fruit of his work./ Jacob ben Solomon died with a good name Tuesday 16 Iyar and was buried on Wednesday the 17th thereof in the year 'You shall be remembered', in his 83rd year. Beneath are deposited the remains of one of the worthies of his native town Plymouth. Jacob Nathan who departed this life the 21 May 5627 [= 1867]. Reader ponder on the memento of a good man. His path during life was upright, just and righteous. The name of Jacob Nathan was proverbial for deeds of kindness and acts of charity to the needy and unfortunate.

Jacob Nathan was the largest single benefactor to the Plymouth Congregation leaving them the bulk of his estate of £13,000. He was a bachelor, first mentioned in Congregational records in 1819, is mentioned in English Goldsmiths as a goldsmith in 1833. His brothers were Nathaniel (b. 1778) and Henry (b. 1793). Their sister Bila died in 183. None married.

B91. Nathan ben Solomon, died Sunday 5 Elul 5625. Nathaniel Nathan died 27 August 5625 [= 1865] aged 87 years.

Brother of Jacob and Henry Nathan.

B92. Missing.

B93. Zvi ben Solomon, died on the Holy Sabbath 23 Tevet 5624 [= 2

January 1864]. Henry Nathan.

Brother of Jacob and Nathaniel Nathan.

B94. Illegible.

B95. ..... in the year 5522 [= 1762].

B96. Illegible.

B97. The upright and worthy Joseph ben Joseph Meir, died Sunday, Rosh Hodesh Heshvan ?5545 [?= 15 October 1784].

He was the Beadle of the Congregation in 1779 and appears to have been a member as early as 1759.

B98. Illegible.

B99. The worthy bachelor Jacob ben .... died 23 Shevat 5523 [= February 1763].

B100. Abraham ben .... died Iyar 5540 [= 1780].

B101. Illegible.

B102. Menahem ben Judah, died Friday, 2 Kislev 5557 [= 2 December 1796].

A deeply incised inscription on slate. The standard abbreviation for 'May his soul be bound up in the bond of life' is at the beginning of the inscription. It is invariably at the end. He and his wife Esther bat Solomon left £2. 2s. to the Synagogue.

B103. Illegible.

B104. Illegible.

B105. Date only - 1804.

B106. Feigala bat Samuel, died 19 Shevat 5628. Reverse: Frances, daughter of Samuel and Phoebe Levy, 12 February 1868.

B107. Brina bat Gershon. Brina, wife of Henry Morris died 28 August 1867, aged 56 years.

Brina Morris (née Joseph, b. Exeter) married Henry or William Morris in 1830. He was born Prussia, a jeweller, of 35 Cambridge Street in 1851. Their children were Cordelia, George, Deborah, Kate, Jacob and Judah.

B108. Brina bat Abraham, died 2 Elul 5625 [= 24 August 1865]. Reverse: Brina Joseph.

Brina Joseph born 1781 Plymouth, daughter of Abraham Joseph I, married Nathan Joseph (Altmann), and had twelve children.

B109. Missing.

B111. Missing.

B112. Here lies a man who went in the path of uprightness, feared God, generous of heart, pursued righteousness and loving kindness and gave to the needy. Abraham ben Eliezer who reached days and years of hoary head and who died on Monday 12th of the month of Ziv [= Iyar], his body lies in the earth but his soul is accepted in the Garden of Eden. He was gathered with great honour to the place of his fathers on Tuesday, the 13th of said month in the year 5632. In memory of Abraham Emdon T.C. Devonport, died 20 May 1872/5632, aged 73 years.

Abraham Emden (b. 1799, Plymouth), son of Eliezer Emden I, married twice, firstly to Martha Frumat and secondly Lydia, daughter of Mordecai Davis. He was a pawnbroker in Cornwall Street, Devonport in 1844, and at 13 Ordnance Street in 1851. Elected Town Councillor of Devonport on 9 November 1870, and a year later was a member of the General Purposes

Committee.

B113. The outstanding Torah scholar, righteous, and upright. Isaac ben Abraham. When he was 73 years old he was called to the Yeshiva on High. 10 Shevat 5732. Isaac Isaacs died 19 January 1872 aged 72(!) years.

Isaac Isaacs (b. Bavaria, 1803) married Fanny (b. Exeter, 1812. Their children were all born in Plymouth: Amelia, Isabella, Nancy, Julia, Jeanette. He was a master jeweller of 31 Frankfurt Street in 1851. In the 1871 census he is described as a general clothes dealer at 1 Abbey Place.

B114. Missing.

B115. Missing.

B116. At the age of ?13 years he ascended to Heaven. The bachelor Ze'ev ben Abraham, in the year ?5610 [= ?1850]. Reverse: Wolf Rosenberg.

B117. Alexander ben Meir, died 19 Av 5629 [= 27 July 1869].

Alexander Klapper (b. 1834) married on 12 November 1862 to Amelia Rain of 8 Leigham Terrace, Plymouth, daughter of Abraham Rain. Klapper was a clothier of 92 Pembroke Street, Devonport in 1862.

B118. Missing.

B119. The righteous man Mordecai ben Jacob, died Friday and was buried on Sunday ... 5567 [= 1806/7.)

Mordecai Jacobs (b. 1727, Prague), landed at Harwich in 1750, spent 3 years in London and was then in Cornwall from 1753-1773. He was an umbrella maker and remained in Plymouth from 1773 until his death on 4 October 1806. In 1805 he lived at 85 Market Place, Plymouth.

B119a. Joseph ben Baruch, died 27 Heshvan 5627 [= 5 November 1866] aged 72 years.

B119b. Hannah Moses.

A broken stone lying on the ground in pieces. According to Revd. Berlin she was the wife of Phillip Moses II, she died Friday, 23 December 1864 aged 83. These details are no longer legible.

B119c. Rose Philip [Berlin read: Rosie Phillips], died 5 January (1803) aged 55 years.

Reizcha bat Samuel SGL, she was a clothes broker of 15 Market Street, Plymouth Dock in 1823. From 1825-1826 she was one of the few women members of the Plymouth Meshivat Nefesh Society.

B120. Illegible or Missing.

B125. Illegible or Missing. Tombstone number A56 (Mrs Reichla Benjamin) lies next to B126.

B126. ... ben Abraham KZ, [died] 55[??].

Priestly hands have been carved at the top.

SECTION C

C1. Abraham Isaac ben Joseph, died 22 Kislev ...

Abraham Joseph I (1731- 24 November 1794), aged 63. Abraham Joseph wholesale dealer in slops for the Navy. 'He amassed a considerable fortune by very fair and honest means'. As an agent for seamen, his practice was well worthy the imitation of every person in that business, as several orphans and indigent widows can testify (Gentleman's Magazine 1794, p. 1156).' He was married to Rosy Abrahams and their children were Phoebe, Esther, Joseph, Brina, Samuel, Aaron, Gella, Henel. Bequeathed numerous properties and dwellings to his family on his death. His scrolls of the Sefer Torah in the Synagogue were to be given one to Joseph, one to Samuel, and the oldest to the 'Synagogue and the Jew people frequenting same'. 'The pair of Aaron silver bells and the plate thereto belonging shall never be sold or alienated from my family'. Joseph's son Henry got a gold watch and silver shoe and stone knee buckles. 'To Moses Ephraim, schoolmaster £12. 12s. 0d. within twelve months to say certain prayers for me daily'. The interest of £100 in the Oakhampton Turnpike to be paid to the Beth Hamidrash in London. 'The interest on £100 for the Synagogue in Plymouth upon condition and in confidence that proper prayers are said for me in the synagogue every Jewish Sabbath Day, and every holiday, and if the people attending at such times shall refuse, neglect, or omit to say such prayers for me, then the executors are to pay the interest to the Institution in London'.

C2. Upon the mountains I will raise my cry and upon the heavens my lamentation [Jer. 9:9] for the young maiden, the daughter of our people Gella bat Abraham known as Arbilai. She died on the Holy Sabbath, 11 Kislev 5574 [= 4 December 1813]. May her soul be bound up in the bond of life.

She was the daughter of Abraham Joseph I.

C3. Illegible.

C4. Illegible.

C5. Joseph ben Abraham Isaac.

Joseph Joseph (1766 - 6 September 1846), son of Abraham Joseph I. Silversmith and slop merchant, continued in his father's footsteps, generous benefactor of the Synagogue. In 1798 he gave a burial plot worth £105 to the Congregation, also an Ark curtain, two golden breastplates and a small cover. He owned extensive property, but lost his money and went bankrupt. He moved in High Society and appears to have been friends with

King William IV when the latter was at Dartmouth in his youth.

C6. Here lies a modest women, precious in her actions, her glory was at home and she was praised without, ninety were the days of the years of her life when she was gathered to her people and to her fathers. She was the benefactress, a woman of worth, Edal bat Abraham Zvi, who died with a good name on Thursday, 11th Adar and was buried here in honour on Friday, the 12th thereof 5621 [= 21 February 1861].

She was the wife of Joseph Joseph. She was born in Liskeard in 1771.

C7. Zvi ben [?] Nahum, died ... ?5552 [= 1792].

C8. Missing.

C9. Illegible.

C10. Illegible.

TRANSCRIPTIONS BY REVD DR M. BERLIN

Original numbering and locations as noted by Dr Berlin have been retained below:

8/6. With bitter cry we bemoan the child Abraham ben Samuel, died on the 2nd day of Shavuot 5564 [= 7 May 1804] aged 5 years.

8/7. The child Isaac ben ?Avigdor/?Abimelech. 5564 [= 1804].

9/10. May he be with the congregation of the upright, there with the sweet voiced may he dwell, the perfect man Moses ben Isaac, Shammash and Trusty of the Holy Congregation of Plymouth. Died and buried on Thursday, 18 Sivan in the year 'and ye shall circumcise the foreskin of your heart' [= 1780].

Moses Isaac (b. 1728, Mezeritz in Poland), moved to Frankfurt, landed in

Harwich 1748. His wife was Dikah bat Jacob and when she died in 1815 the stock which she left was sold to satisfy the expenses incurred by the Congregation on her behalf. Isaac was appointed as Teacher of children in 1781 though he probably acted in this capacity at an earlier date because he signed the minutes of the congregation as Beadle in 1778.

10/2. A woman of worth Golda bat Judah, died and buried Sunday, 19 Adar Rishon 5559 [= 24 February 1799].

10/3. With bitter cries we mourn the child Elijah ben Abraham, died and buried on Sunday, 9 Adar Sheni 5527 [= 10 March 1767].

10/4. The generous Israel ben Jacob, died 29 Adar Rishon 5559 [= 5 April 1799].

Israel Jacobs (b. 1743, Oberhausen, Germany). Landed in Harwich in 1762. He was a silversmith in Southside Street, Plymouth. A member of the Congregation in 1767, subscribed one guinea in 1779 for the Plymouth Congregation's War Levy, and one guinea in 1782 for a new Scroll of the Law. He was probably a brother of Nathan Jacobs of Dartmouth.

10/5. Naphtali Hirtz ben Benjamin, died on Friday, 4 Iyar and was buried on Sunday 5561 [= 17 April 1801] aged 75.

Naphtali Benjamin (b. Ilbersheim, near Mannheim, 1725). Landed at Harwich in 1745, and appears to have settled in Plymouth by 1759. He acted as beadle in 1778, and was a boxmaker shortly before his death.

10/6. An upright man, a righteous priest, who helped the poor, to services he went morning and night, Federale ben Abraham KZ. Died and buried with a good name on Wednesday, 13th Adar Sheni 5562 [= 17 March 1802].

11/2. My heart weeps for the praised woman, wife of Lapidot [Judges 4:4]

Gittla bat Michael, wife of the late Zalman Mannheimer, who died on 4 Iyar 5565 [= 3 May 1805].

Her husband was Solomon Zalman ben Abraham KZ Mannheimer who was a member some time before 1782.

13/7. Nathan ben Jacob from Dartmouth, died Friday 14 Heshvan 5592 [= 24 October 1831].
Reverse: Nathan Jacobs, late of Dartmouth, 6 November 5592 [sic].

Nathan Jacobs was a member of the Plymouth Congregation before 1779 when he made a big disturbance in the Synagogue for which he had to make an abject apology. He was a jeweller in Dartmouth. His wife was Miriam and their children were Alexander, Angel, Betsy, Martha and Zipporah. By his will he appointed Arthur Bailey Harris, a banker, and Alexander as executors of his estate which amounted to some thousands of pounds.

13/7b. Yehiel ben Naphtali, died and buried Wednesday, 3 Nisan 5581 [= 5 April 1821].

Possibly he was Henry Hart, the father of Moses Hart. In Plymouth before 1805.

13/10. Judah ben Moses Jacob, died [or was buried] the eve of Rosh Hodesh Shevat 5586 [= 8 January 1826] aged 87 years.

Judah Moses I (b. 1741, Hartheim in Wurzburg) landed 1763 in Harwich and came straight to Plymouth. His daughter Esther married Alexander ben Samuel of Truro. Judah played an important part in the affairs of the Congregation in the early nineteenth century. He subscribed to the Plymouth Congregation's War Levy of 1779. He was insured as a watchmaker, silversmith and slopseller at 62 Southside Street, Plymouth in 1805.

13/12. Ezekiel Judah ben the late Abraham, died 15 Tevet 5583 [= 29 December 1822.]

13/13. Simha ben Isaac the Levite who was called Bunam Segal died Monday 25 Tevet 5579 [= 25 January 1819.) The Parnas and Manhig of the Holy Congregation of Plymouth, aged 53 years.

Benjamin Levy (b. 1776, Hamelburg, Germany) landed in London 1782, and spent 4 years in Arundel, came to Plymouth in 1786. He was insured as a silversmith, haberdasher and optician at 47 Market Street, Plymouth from 1800. On 1 April 1816 he signed as B. Levy in English characters and Bunam in Hebrew, slopseller, a lease for water for a house in Portland Square inhabited by John Tubby. One of the first Jews to be listed in the Devon Directory, he was an optician in Southside Street until his death in 1819. A ewer and basin are carved at the top of the stone.

13/14. Baruch ben Isaac Moses, died on the eve of Rosh Hodesh Shevat 5577 [= 17 January 1871] aged 35 years.

Barrow Moss of Devonport. Berlin says that there was poetry on the reverse, but did not record it. Barrow's wife was Sally, whose father Solomon Isaac came to Plymouth in 1776 and left her a fortune of about £1,500. The Congregation still uses a silver besomim box (spice holder used in the havdalah ceremony at the conclusion of the Sabbath) which his widow presented originally to the Plymouth Dock Minyan.

13/15. Mordecai ben Abraham, died Friday, 21 Heshvan 5572 [= 8 November 1811].

Mordecai Abraham (b. 1743, Gelheim) arrived in England via Harwich 1766, and in 1803 was a silversmith at 37 St Andrews Street, Plymouth. He died at North Corner Street, Plymouth Dock. In his will he is described as a shopkeeper and licenced hawker. His wife was Rachel, and their children were Abraham, Judah, Rebecca and Phoebe.

13/16. Jacob ben Mordecai, and was gathered to his forefathers on Wednesday, 2nd day of Rosh Hodesh Elul and was buried on Friday ?10 Elul.

Jacob Jacob. The son of Mordecai Jacob who landed in England in 1750. He was insured as a silversmith and toyman of Market Place, Plymouth, from 3 February 1796. He remained there until his death. His will leaves 'to the Jewish synagogue at Plymouth, of which I am by the blessing of God a member, £100 to be invested in 5% annuities, the interest to be given to the poor Jews of Plymouth every year in Elul, on condition that my late father Mordecai Jacobs, and myself, be commemorated forever at the Yizkor service. In default of which my heirs are to sue the congregation in payment of £100. £10 towards ten poor people for making a competent meeting for prayers every Saturday, and £5 to Mr Ephraim to say a certain portion of the Holy Scriptures as a prayer for me on every Saturday, £5 to my brother in law, Rabbi Simon for saying a prayer called Kaddish [mourner's prayer] for me in the synagogue every day, a mourning ring to each of my nephews and the residue to my dearly beloved wife Hannah Jacobs, daughter of Hayim Barnett of the City of Gloucester.'

13/17. The old man Solomon ben Nathan, died on the Holy Sabbath 15 Shevat 5571 [= 9 February 1811].

Solomon Nathan (b. 1740, Merionthal, Germany), landed Harwich 1756 and came straight to Plymouth where he had family. Father of Jacob, Henry, Nathaniel and Bila Nathan. His wife was Rachel was sister of Abraham Daniel, a noted miniaturist. He was a goldsmith, and apparently the only registered Jewish master who took registered apprentices in the South West. Judah Lyons was apprenticed to him in 1772 for £42.

O8. My wife Feigela bat Mordecai, wife of Isaac ben Avigdor, died on account of the plague, Tuesday, 2nd day of Rosh Hodesh Elul 5592 [= 28 August 1832]. Reverse: Fanny, wife of S. Lyon.

First wife of Solomon Lyon. She was a straw hat maker in Pyke Street in 1822.

O10. Esther bat Abraham from the State of Poland, the Holy Congregation of Lublin, died 25 Tevet 5591 [= 7 January 1831].

The wife of Lazarus Solomon, possibly his first wife.

O11. (Jose) Cohen, she died 2 April 5589 [= 1829] aged 3 months.

O12. Sarah bat David the Priest, died 15 Heshvan 5581 [= 23 October 1820].

O13. An elder, honoured and respected, who attained 80 years like a mighty man. He ran like a hart and was as swift as an eagle to do that which was right and upright, the scholar Sampson ben Nathan, who died on Tuesday, 27 Iyar 5577 [= 13th May 1817] the 42nd day of the Omer according to the counting of the children of Israel. May he arise in his turn at the time appointed which is sealed in the Book.

Simon Nathan (b. 1747 near Marienbad in Bohemia), landed at Harwich in 1773 and came straight to Plymouth where he was a dealer and chapman at 85 Market Place in 1803. As early as 1786, he was in a comfortable way of life, able to have water piped into his house on the conduit system.

O16. Nencha bat Yehie[l], wife of the late Zvi ben Nathan, died 15 Heshvan 5574 [= 8 November 1813].

O17. Brina bat Solomon known as Zalman KZ, wife of Reuben known as Zelig, died Tuesday 21 Kislev 5574 [= 14 December 1813].

Mrs Brina Isaacs, the wife of Solomon Isaacs.

O18. The elder, Reuben Zelig ben Isaac, died the Holy Sabbath 21 Kislev

5576 [= 23 December 1815]. *Solomon Isaac (b. 1751 in Mannheim) landed in London 1775, arrived in Plymouth 1776, a silversmith, noted in the Devon Directories from 1798, a tenant of one of Joseph Joseph's houses in Southside Street. His wife was Brina, or Briney. By his will he appointed Leviah, wife of Levy Zachariah, Sally, wife of Barrow Moss, Isaac Isaacs, three of his children, to be executors of his estate which was sworn at £3,000.*

O21. Minnela bat Menahem, wife of the Parnas and Manhig Zvi ben Samuel who went to her rest on Sunday, 25 Heshvan and was buried on the 28th thereof 5572 [= 12 November 1811].

She was the wife of Henry Hart, who in 1797 was one of the Trustees of the synagogue.

O22. The bachelor Abraham ben Nathan, Dartmouth, died on the Holy Sabbath, the eve of Shavuot, and was buried on Isru Hag 5572 [= 16 May 1812] aged 20 years.

A son of Nathan Jacobs of Dartmouth.

O23. The child Miriam bat Yehiel, died on Friday, 6 Elul 5572 [= 14 August 1812].

P7. Moses Isaac ben Judah, died Friday and buried Sunday 14 Elul 5593 [= 2 September 1833].

Isaac Moses, known as Ike Moses, probably a son of Judah Moses I who came to Plymouth in 1763.

P16. The Parnas and Manhig Yehiel Michael ben Zvi, died Thursday, 20 Adar 5579 [= 17 March 1819].

Michael Hart (b. 1739 near Mannheim) came to England via Harwich in 1763. A silversmith in Howes Lane in 1803.

P17. Alexander Aryeh ben Menahem, died 14 Heshvan 5579 [= 16 November 1818], with hoary head and full of days.

P18. Edal bat Samuel, wife of Alexander Aryeh ben Menahem, died Sunday, 9 Heshvan 5579 [= 8 November 1818], aged 65 years.

His surname was Emanuel, his children were Samuel, Ezekiel and Menahem.

P20. Genella bat Baruch, wife of the late Joseph ben Zvi, from the Holy Congregation of Falmouth, died Friday, 9 Kislev 5577 [= 29 November 1816].

Q5. The child Miriam bat Jacob, Betsy Miriam Jacob, daughter of the late Lewis Jacobs.

Q6. Judah ben Isaac, died 8 Sivan 5600 [= 7 June 1840]. Reverse: Lewis Jacobs; 7 June 1840, aged 49 years.

Lewis Jacobs I, goldsmith in 1823 in Totnes.

Q16. The bachelor Issachar ben Joel, died 25 Shevat 5582 [= 16 February 1822].

Q19. The bachelor Aaron ben Simeon the Levite, died 13 Tishri 5579 [= 13 October 1818].

The stone has an ewer and basin at the top.

Q24. Joshua Falk ben the late Isaac from Breslau. He was slain in the place of Fowey by the uncircumcised and impure man Wyatt and drowned in the waters, 14 Kislev 5572 and buried on the 17th thereof [= 30 November 1811], aged 26 years.

Isaac Valentine who acted as an agent for the Josephs, a Plymouth family, who in turn were acting on behalf of the London bankers Goldsmid, who were buying up golden guineas for the Government. He was enticed to bring £260 to Fowey by an innkeeper called Wyatt and was murdered by him and dropped into the dock. Wyatt was hanged for this crime at Bodmin in the presence of a large crowd which flocked in from all the countryside.

Q25. Zadok ben Asher, died 5 Tamuz 5570 [= 7 July 1810].

R8. Joseph ben Zvi, died 16 Adar Rishon 5603 [= 16 February 1843]

R15. Abraham ben Isaac, died Monday, 5 Tishri 5585 [= 27 September 1824].

Abraham Isaac, born 1741 Furth, landed at Harwich in 1761, and was an old clothes dealer in Southside Street in 1803. In the Congregational records he is always described as Abraham ben Isaac Schnapfuchs.

R22. The Torani Aaron ben Michael, died 10 Av [followed by the chronogram] 'According to the counting of the children of Israel' [= ?1753 or ?1813].

R24. The bachelor Issachar Behrman ben Joshua Levy the righteous Priest from the Holy Congregation of London, died ?Yom Kippur 5565 [= 15 September 1804] in the Island of Madeira, and was buried here in Plymouth on Friday, the eve of Sabbath, Iyar 5565 [= May 1805].

The Plymouth Congregation has a silver bowl and jug for the use of the Priests given by his family in gratitude for 'the loving kindness done to the bones of our son'.

S1. A most exalted man Menahem ben Isaac from London who laboured .... he died on Monday and was buried on Tuesday..... Av 5580 [= ? July 1820]. Emanuel Levy.

He might be Levy Emanuel (AL30) who was born in 1732 in Weisendorf, Germany, and came to Truro via Harwich in 1748. He was a silversmith in Plymouth from 1763, and in Frankfort Place, Plymouth, in 1803. There was an Emanuel Levy who came from Jamaica and died and was buried in Plymouth in July 1825. A Mr Simons of Falmouth laid out £20 to cover the cost of his burial.

S3. Joseph ben Naphtali, died and buried on Wednesday 13 Tamuz 5559 [= 16 July 1799].

Joseph Henry (AL48), born 1735, Sandfelt, came to England via Harwich in 1766, was a clothes dealer in Lower Lane.

S6. Joseph ben Jacob Mannheim called Yosepha Mannheimer, died Sunday, 24 Sivan 5582 [= 11 June 1822].

Joseph Hart (b. 1756, Mannheim) came to Plymouth via Harwich in 1770 and was a silversmith at 35 Market Street, Plymouth. He left Plymouth between 1798 and 1803, but returned to lodgings. He died, and four banknotes of £100 each, gold and silver coins, as well as much gold and silver to a total value of £700 or £800 were found in his lodgings by his landlord William Pyne, who at first refused to hand over the effects. The Congregation appointed a committee of four men to take steps to recover the property and administer it for the benefit of the heirs.

S9. David ben Moses from Norwich, died and was buried 23 Heshvan 5573 [= 29 October 1812].

David Moses born 1737 near Saarbruck, landed in Harwich in 1759 and moved straight to Norwich where he traded as a spectacle maker until 1793, when he moved to Plymouth. In 1803 he lived in Southside Street.

T1. My husband Isaac Eliezer ben Sampson, died the first Intermediate Day of Succot 5611 [= 23 September 1850].

The old Jewish cemetery, the Hoe

Section B of the old Jewish cemetery

Section C visible in the foreground (lower part)

SECTION 5

Jewish Cemetery, Gifford Place

Plymouth

When further expansion was required for burials in 1868 a plot of land was acquired in the Compton Gifford area of Plymouth. The land was purchased by Plymouth Hebrew Congregation and a proper chapel erected. The first internment in the cemetery was of Councillor William Woolf on 3 December 1872. Since then, over a period of some 140 years, there have been over 750 burials. A complete burial register does not appear to exist for the site, although two versions of a large cemetery plan, with the names of those buried here, does exist. The plans have aided a fuller list to be completed here when added to surveys carried out by the late Rabbi Dr Bernard Susser in the 1960s and the author, Dr Helen Fry, in the late 1990s. As of August 2012 there are no burials in Sections BE, BF, BG. The cemetery is one of the few Jewish cemeteries outside London which has its own caretaker's lodge and called Jews' Cemetery Lodge.

Views of the cemetery

Burials in the Gifford Place cemetery:

ROW A

1. MYER ISAAC ROSEMAN, 15 February 1935, aged 68, husband of Amelia
2. MYER FREDMAN, 5 August 1927, aged 57, 'honoured citizen of his native…'
3. LEVIN FREDMAN, 18 October 1912, aged 68
4. WILLIAM WOLFE, 1 February 1873, aged 63
5. S WOLFE, 2 April 1874, aged 26
6. SON OF JUDAH WOLFE, 1874
7. A NELSON, 10 February 1874, aged 45
8. RALPH CORREA, 26 April 1875, interesting inscription
9. HENRY MORRIS, 19 December 1875
10. Unknown
11. RICHARD KAUFMAN, June 1879, aged 66
12. ASHER JOEL, 1 September 1880, aged 70
13. SIGMUND YAGER, 2 April 1882, aged 65
14. 10 May 1883, English inscription illegible
15. ABRAHAM JACOBS, 5 March 1886
16. EZRA NATHAN, 1 January 1894, aged 74
17. PHILIP BLOOM, 14 February 1934, aged 59
18. FRANK HOLDENBERG, 23 May 1934, aged 54
19. MYER ROSEMAN, 5 February 1936, aged 56, husband of Lena
20. TOBIAS BRAND, 16 February 1936, aged 71
21. MR STONE, 11 July 1936
22. ISAAC FORMAN, 27 July 1936, aged 59
23. ALEXANDER GOLDSTEIN, 6 February 1937, aged 25
24. HARRY BROCK, 15 March 1937, aged 76

25. CHARLES BASS, 22 April 1937, aged 48

26. MR H. PRICE, 21 December 1937

27. MORRIS SMITH, 11 may 1946, aged 61, husband of Sadie (Sarah)

28. ALFRED BROCK, 10 July 1946, aged 81

29. SAMUEL W SELWOOD, 2 April 1947, aged 39

30. ERNEST HYMAN CAPLAN, 19 November 1949, aged 49, eldest son of Leah & late Abraham Caplan

ROW B

1. FANNY KAPLAN, 29 July 1929, aged 25

2. RACHEL ROSEMAN, 3 March 1928, aged 80, widow of Israel Roseman

3. REBECCA FREDMAN, 3 July 1919, aged 43

4. HETTY FREDMAN, 22 February 1910, aged 77, widow of Aryeh Eliezer Fredman

5. Unknown

6. FANNY LYONS, 1873, aged 78

7. Unknown

8. AMELIA RALPH, 26 November 1874, aged 62

9. JULIA LEVY, 31 December 1874, aged 54

10. GELA LEVI, 10 April 1875, aged 54

11. Unknown

12. BELLA LEVI, 16 April 1878

13. MARIA MITCHELL, 25 April 1879, aged 74

14. HANNAH JOSEPH, 25 May 1879, aged 74

15. HARRIET JACOBS, 28 August 1879, aged 69, wife of Alexander Jacobs

16. ESTER ISRAEL, 18 April 1880, stone fallen and broken

17. CHAYA SARAH COHEN, 20 March 1891, aged 80

18. BERNARD BAUN, 12 June 1938, aged 71

19. LOUIS GOLDSTEIN, 10 February 1939

20. HARRIS BENCE, 9 March 1939, aged 76

21. AARON ERNEST ROSEMAN, 17 March 1939, aged 66

22. HYMAN LIPMAN, 10 October 1939, aged 40

23. ABRAHAM ISAAC ERLICH, 6 January 1940, aged 59

24. SAMUEL ERLICH, 28 January 1940

25. ALEXANDER VERNON JONAS, 5 June 1940

26. DAVID JONAS, 6 July 1941, husband of Bertha Jonas

27. ISAAC LAZARUS, 30 July 1946, aged 80

28. CHARLES SOLOMON BROCK, 13 March 1947, aged 83

29. LOUIS ROBINS, 22 January 1948, aged 73

30. MR BOLTON, 6 December 1949

31. SOLOMON PEARL, 26 January 1950, aged 83

ROW C

1. BERT ROSEMAN, 2 January 1911, aged 26, son of Rachel & Israel Roseman

2. ISRAEL ROSEMAN, 16 October 1910, husband of Rachel Roseman

3. SAMUEL JACOBS, 12 June 1884, aged 84

4. HENRY WOLFE, 14 April 1881

5. LOUIS ZEITUNG (GABRIELSON), 16 August 1886, aged 19, eldest son of Morris & Henrietta Gabrielson

6. LEON ISAAC, 7 May 1887, aged 48

7. LEWIS HYMAN, 16 June 1888

8. ISAAC NEWMAN, 27 May 1889

9. Unknown

10. ABRAHAM RALPH, 4 October 1890, aged 76

11. ABRAHAM JACOBS, 29 October 1890, aged 62, formerly of Exeter

12. ALEXANDER JACOBS, 13 August 1893, aged 86, of Paignton & Torquay

13. AARON WOLFE, 17 February 1890, husband of Phoebe Wolf

14. BARNETT LYONS, 2 April 1888, aged 70

15. LEVI FREDMAN, 17 January 1886, aged 54

16. CALMEN WINEBERG, 1 September 1884

17. JACOB FREDMAN, 2 December 1898, aged 64

18. MARY SMITH, 10 July 1940, aged 72, killed by enemy action

19. ESTHER SMITH, 10 July 1940, aged 38 – double stone with C18

20. SALLIE STOLLER, 23 October 1940, aged 39

21. MRS MATHILDA PHILLIPS, 18 November 1940, aged 53

22. BERTHA SPERLING, 30 September 1941, aged 82, widow of Samuel Sperling

23. ANNIE ERLICH, 6 August 1946, aged 63

24. MRS ROSE

25. MISS PAULINE SILVERSTONE, 20 March 1943, aged 31

26. JANE WEINBERG, 7 March 1943, aged 76

27. FLORA PEARL, 1 September 1943, aged 67

28. RAY WOLFSON, 18 November 1943

29. CAROLINE ALBERTA LEAH BROCK, 25 January 1944, aged 79

30. PAMELA ROBINS, 3 March 1944, aged 22, only daughter of Louis & Lulu Robins

31. LULU ROBINS, 7 December 1954, aged 62

ROW D

1. LIBBY ROBINS, 4 September 1919, aged 69

2. ABIGAIL NATHAN, 20 December 1894

3. MRS P LEVI, 17 November 1880, aged 71

4. SARAH NEWMAN, 5 February 1881

5. RACHEL BAUM, 30 October 1882, wife of Philip Baum, born Germany September 1833
6. SARAH BROCK, 5 January 1884
7. PHOEBE SHEPPERD, 28 April 1884, aged 35
8. HENRIETTA SUSMAN, 15 November 1884
9. Unknown
10. ESTHER LEVI, 31 December 1895, aged 74
11. MISS BETSY ALEXANDER, 1 December 1886, aged 86
12. JANETTE SAMUELS, 3 march 1888, aged 67
13. JULIA BASCH, 8 April 1888, aged 58
14. MISS BLOOMEY ALEXANDER, 1 September 1889, aged 81
15. FANNY ISAACS, 8 December 1889, aged 77
16. JANE ELIZABETH LYONS, 25 February 1890, aged 65
17. JANE LYONS, 25 February 1890
18. RACHEL FREDMAN, 28 January 1922, aged 84, widow of Jacob
19. HARRIS NATHAN, 8 November 1940, aged 70
20. ELIJAH BARKE, 4 December 1940, aged 62
21. MAURICE SANGER, 14 July 1941, aged 53
22. MORRIS, 20 October 1941
22. BARNETT COHEN, 17 May 1942, aged 83
23. MORRIS SOLOMON, 21 July 1942 (402679, Sgt of Royal Australian Air Force)
24. MORTON MORRIS, 23 October 1942, aged 46
25. JACOB GREENBURGH, 23 November 1942, aged 86
26. MICHAEL SOLOMON, 7 January 1943, aged 62
27. JOSEPH GREENBURGH, 30 September 1943, aged 56
28. JOSEPH MILNER, 5 April 1944, aged 61
29. NATHAN CHARLES, 15 October 1944, aged 65

30. JOSEPH (JACK) GORDON, 17 December 1944, aged 61, of St Austell

31. ABRAHAM LEVY, 17 February 1945

ROW E

1. GEDALIA MORDECAI ROBINS, 7 December 1907, aged 59
2. S. FREDMAN, 25 March 1899, aged 78
3. Unknown
4. HERMAN LONDON, 4 January 1894, aged 48
5. ELIJAH MYER SONNENBERG, January 1894, aged 47
6. WOLFE JACOB ULLMAN, 26 January 1894, aged 59
7. MOSELY JOEL, 9 April 1895, 39 (born 12 August 1855)
8. LOUIS CONITZ [stone down], 24 July 1895
9. VICTOR LIEPA ROTH, 1 February 1896, aged 13, son of Benjamin & Bertha Roth
10. ROSALIA SIMPSON, 13 July 1890, aged 6 months
11. Unknown
12. Unknown
13. DORA SARA DEBORAH SIMPSON, 1 January 1896, aged 1 year 10 months
14. Unknown
15. LEAH ROSEMAN, 5 January 1897, aged 16 months, infant of Israel & Rachel Roseman
16. HANNAH SARAH ROSEMAN, 10 June 1897, aged 2 months, daughter of Myer Isaac & Amelia Roseman
17. AMELIA MANDELSTAM, 30 April 1892, relict of Emil Mandelstam, eldest daughter of Isaacs of Plymouth
18. FRANCIS NATHAN, 29 October 1896
19. Unknown

20. RALPH ENJAMIN EMDON, 10 February 1944, aged 25, ex-Sgt of Queens Royal Regiment
21. SAMUEL ISAAC OWEN, 10 September 1945, aged 68, husband of Rebecca Sarah Owen
22. ABRAHAM (BOBBY) ROBINS, 12 October 1945, aged 77, husband of Rose
23. LEWIS LADDEN, 31 May 1946, aged 71
24. SOLOMON GORDON, 3 October 1947, aged 62
25. BARNETT MELICHAN, 21 June 1948, aged 55
26. ELY MYER AZERMAN, 7 February 1950, husband of Winifred
27. Void
28. Void
29. ABRAHAM SILVERSTONE, 6 May 1952, aged 78
30. HYMAN JOHN NELSON, 24 January 1952
31. ISIDORE COHEN, 29 December 1950, aged 70, husband of Phoebe Cohen
32. JOSEPH SPARK, 2 October 1950, aged 73, husband of Augusta
33. ERNEST BROCK, 11 February 1950 (???), aged 77, husband of Lilian Ada Brock

ROW F

1. LIEBA FREDMAN, 15 May 1919, aged 100, widow of Samuel Wolf Fredman
2. REBECCA EMDEN, 9 March 1895, aged 79, widow of Wolf Emden
3. Unknown
4. ESTHER NELSON, 17 March 1891, aged 39, wife of J.S Nelson
5. HARRIET BELLEM, 28 October 1890, aged 80
6. HANNAH ISAACS, 26 October 1890, aged 72
7. MATILDA HANNAH WINEBERG, 27 march 1890, aged 28

8. ROSE JOEL, 6 March 1890, aged 77, relict of Asher Joel

9. PHOEBE WOLF, 23 June 1894, aged 73, wife of Aron Wolf

10. EDITH ROSE EMDEN, 2 July 1886

11. Unknown

12. Unknown

13. Unknown

14. Unknown

15. Unknown

16. Unknown

17. BARNET GOODMAN, 18 May 1890

18. FRANCES NATHAN, 29 October 1896, aged 73, daughter of Lionel Nathan

19. Unknown

20. EDITH BLANCHE LANGNER, 1 November 1945

21. FANNY HARRIS, 26 December 1946, aged 63, wife of Saul Harris

22. ESTHER SCHULMAN, 5 April 1946, aged 85

23. FRUMA LEMPERT, 17 January 1947, aged 81, born Palestine

24. HETTY BARKE, 19 May 1947, aged 72

25. HANNAH BROCK, 15 August 1947, aged 82

26. ANNIE ROBBINS, 5 November 1947, aged 49

27. LENA ROSEMAN, 9 November 1947, aged 66, widow of Myer Roseman

28. MRS STONE, 3 June 1948

29. RACHEL LESKIN, 5 June 1948, aged 57

30. CHARLOTTE ESTHER LAURENCE, 12 January 1949, aged 76

31. REBECCA SILVERSTONE, 17 December 1949, aged 76

32. GERTRUDE AUGUSTA BLOOM, 6 April 1949, aged 72

33. LILIAN ADA (CISSIE) BROCK, 20 May 1978, aged 92, widow of Ernest Brock

ROW G

1 – 9. Twelve unknown children

10. SAMUEL LAZARUS, 18 September 1890, aged 11 months, son of Isaac & Jane Lazarus

11. Unknown

12. Unknown

13. ABRAHAM ORGEL, 16 December 1893

14. Unknown

15. Unknown

16. Unknown

17. BARNETT GOODMAN, 18 May 1890, aged 9 months

18. Baby SILVERSTONE, 1946

19. Baby LEWIS, 1946

21- 26. Unknown

27. JANEY LAZARUS, 3 February 1951, aged 85, widow of Isaac Lazarus

ROW H

1. Unknown

2. Unknown

3. Unknown

4. Unknown

5. Unknown

6. ESTHER FREDMAN, 1883

7-12. Unknown

13. Baby FREYA GORDON, 6 June 1949

Above division path:

14. Unknown

15. Unknown

16. RAYNOR TUCHMAN, 13 June 1954, aged 86

17. ROSE LEWIS, 31 March 1954, aged 78

18. CATHERINE BISHOP, 3 February 1954, aged 90

19. MIRIAM FRANCES BROCK, 27 December 1953, aged 58, wife of John

20. CISSIE PHYLLIS GOODMAN, 27 April 1952, aged 44, wife of Jack Goodman

21. HETTIE SANGER, 21 March 1952, aged 67

22. CLARA ABRAHAMS, 4 June 1951, aged 65

23. AMELIA ROSEMAN, 10 January 1951, aged 51, widow of Myer Isaac Roseman

28. MIRIAM HANNAH BRAND, 22 June 1950, aged 87

29. FANNY FREDMAN, 31 March 1950, aged 96, widow of Myer Fredman

30. REBECCA CHARLES, 8 March 1950, aged 74

31. ESTHER ABRAHAMS, 8 December 1949

ROW J

1. LOUIS ROSEMAN, 2 May 1902, aged 7½, son of Myer Isaac & Amelia Roseman

2. Unknown

3. REBECCA MINDEL PEARL, 18 December 1904

4. NATHAN JOSEPH, 20 December 1904, aged 11

5. Unknown

6. SAMUEL BENJAMIN PEARL, 11 January 1905, aged 8 years & 1 month

7. BERTHA ROBINS, 20 February 1906, aged 9, eldest daughter of Abraham & Rose Robins

8. EVA JACOBS, 17 July 1906, aged 3½, daughter of Revd D & Mrs Jacobs
9. Unknown
Division path
10. Unknown
11. ROSY COHEN, 4 December 1898, aged 10½ months, daughter of Barnett & Sarah Cohen

12 -18. Ten unknown children, amongst which appears to be buried HERMIONE CONICK, 13 May 1938

19. LOUIS GRAHAM ROBINS, 24 February 1953, aged 2 & 9 months, son of Gerald & Rita Robins
20. Baby STEIN, 19 September 1953
21. REV EMMANUEL GOODMAN, 17 March 1959, aged 62
22. JOSHUA HURWITT, 3 September 1959, aged 62
23. JOHN (JACOB NATHAN) BROCK, 13 March 1959, aged 91
24. ALOOF, HYMAN, 13 July 1959, aged 72: '*He occupied himself in faithfulness with the wants of the congregation*'. Beadle and Reader of Plymouth synagogue, 1924. Sons: Sidney, Lionel and Percy Aloof
25. ABRAHAM EPHRAIM MILNER, 30 December 1958, aged 77
26. MR KINGFIELD, 20 October 1958
27. ABRAHAM ABRAHAMS, 7 October 1957, aged 75
28. MORRIS SALTER, 7 November 1956, aged 43, husband of Annie
29. BLACK, HARRY, 25 January 1956, aged 56
30. SAMUEL LOUIS GOLDBERG, 31 January 1956, aged 84
31. HYMAN SOLOMON (SOLLY) OWEN, 4 November 1955, aged 78, wife of Rose

ROW K

1. DAPHNE IRIS JORDAN, 25 October 1914, aged 4½, daughter of David & Elizabeth Jordan
2. Unknown
3. Unknown
4. (Baby) KALISHER, 7 April 1940
5. Unknown
6. RACHAEL GNOBBOK,
7. MILLY SLAVINSKY, 1 November 1912, aged 3, daughter of Rev & Mrs Slavinsky
8. FANNY GREENBURGH, 24 January 1911, aged 11 years & 9 months, daughter of Jacob & Betsy Greenburgh
9. HARRY CRONENBURG, 17 November 1909, child, English illegible
Division Path
10. MYER FREDMAN, 6 January 1927, aged 71, husband of Fanny Fredman
11. ABRAHAM COHEN, 23 August 1927, aged 82
12. LAWRENCE LEVY, 4 July 1930, aged 43
13. SAULPHINEAS LEMPERT, 12 August 1932, aged 69, husband of Fruma Lempert
14. HENRY COHEN, 3 November 1932, aged 22, son of Isidore and Phoebe Cohen
15. ELIEZAR GREENBURGH, 29 December 1932, aged 60
16. HARRY ROGERS, 12 July 1932
17. MAX BISHOP, 7 October 1928, aged 69
18. MAURICE BURNS, 29 September 1928, aged 40
19. HENRY ISAACS, 6 May 1927
20. Unknown
Narrow gap

23. BELLA GOLDSTEIN, 8 December 1958, aged 74

24. Reserved MRS BLACK

25. JEANNIE RICHMAN, 24 September 1970, aged 77

26. Reserved MRS SALTER

27. ELLEN GOODMAN, 15 June 1957, aged 83

28. KING FIELD, 19 October 1958, aged 77

29. RACHEL GOLD, 5 April 1956, aged 64

30. JANET LADDEN, 5 October 1955, aged 79

31. MINNIE (AMELIA) LAZARUS, 1 July 1955, aged 70

32. NELLIE BROCK, 26 April 1955, aged 60

33. FREYDA ROSEMAN, 22 April 1955, aged 60

34. ETHEL LILIAN (LEAH) CAPLAN, 26 February 1955, aged 73

ROW L

1. Unknown

2. Unknown

3. BERTHA ROTH, 20 December 1931, wife of Benjamin Roth

4. ELLEN AUGUSTA BROCK, 8 January 1932

5. JULIA ISAACS, 23 July 1932, aged 84

6. BECK

7. LEAH PERLA MILNER, 31 August 1933, aged 46

8. SARAH MILNER, 17 November 1933, aged 75

9. REBECCA BENCE, 27 July 1934, aged 76

10. BESSIE GOLDSTEIN, 26 November 1934, aged 44

11. HESTER ROBINS, 5 January 1936

Division Path

12. BESSIE GREENBURGH, 24 September 1936, aged 74

13. SARAH COHEN, 24 January 1932, aged 70, wife of Barnett Cohen

14. HINDA ROSEMAN, 22 May 1937

15. ROSE ALEXANDER, 15 June 1937

16. RACHEL DINA COPLANS, 1 December 1937, aged 78

17. BEENY SILK, 31 May 1938, aged 64

18. ABIGAIL JACOBS, 10 June 1938, aged 59, daughter of late Mark & Henrietta Jacobs

19. ANNIE RACHEL YOUNGLESON, 23 July 1938, aged 73

20. LEAH DEBORAH WOOLFSON, 11 August 1939, aged 66

21. ESTHER GOLDBERG, 11 December 1939, aged 59

22. Unknown BABY, 25 March 1957

Gap

27. ESTHER BLACK, 7 September 1967, aged 72

28.

29. EVA HOLCENBERG, 12 December 1956, aged 75

Gap

ROW M

1. DAVID DANIEL HIRSCH, 25 April 1927, aged, 43, son of late Leah & Woolf Hirsch

2. ABRAM LEVIN, 20 April 1927

3. LEWIS FORMAN, 4 April 1927

4. MAURICE SIMON

5. SILK, 7 January 1926

6. ABRAHAM SAMUEL CAPLAN, 17 October 1925, aged 51

7. MICHAEL JACOBS, 17 September 1925, aged 65, husband of Rachel Jacobs

8. JOSEPH FREEMAN, October 1924

9. SAMUEL SPERLING, 2 September 1924, aged 76

10. HARRIS GOODMAN, 30 August 1924

11. ALFRED NELSON, 19 December 1923, aged 44

Division Path

12. MYER SILVERSTONE, 9 July 1923, aged 78

13. SAMUEL BASH, 5 July 1923, aged 58, husband of Rachel, father of Esther, Miriam, Leah, Eva

14. ABRAHAM COSTA, 8 June 1923

15. ARTHUR PEARL, 13 March 1923, aged 27

16. ABRAHAM CONICK, 29 November 1922, aged 61

17. JOSEPH LYONS, 11 August 1921, aged 78

18. ISAAC ABRAHAMS, 13 October 1920, aged 33

19. JACOB SAMUEL JACOBS, 16 March 1920

20. GUS BASCH, 11 November 1919, aged 67

21. LEWIS LAZARUS, 7 August 1919 (born 9 August 1844)

Gap

22. JOSEPH LEWIS, 6 April 1955 (???), aged 80

23. JOSEPH SANGER, 30 December 1954, aged 69

24. ASHER TUCHMAN, 8 December 1954, aged 87

25. DAVID JORDAN, 1 October 1954, aged 78

26. MORRIS RICHMAN, 9 September 1954, aged 63, husband of Jeannie

27. HENRY LAURENCE, 28 August 1954, aged 83

28. JOSEPH ABRAHAMS, 9 June 1954, aged 66

29. LEO SILVERSTONE, 22 February 1954, aged 70

30. LEWIS GEORGE BROCK, 3 February 1954, aged 62, son of late Alfred & Hannah Brock

31. ELEAZAR BARKE, 28 January 1954, aged 73

32. CECIL ISRAEL BRAND, 2 September 1953, aged 55

33. ERNEST AARON ROBINS, 22 May 1953, aged 80

ROW N

1. CORDELIA MORRIS, 23 February 1910

2. Unknown

3. ANNIE PRICE, 12 February 1918, wife of Isaac Price

4. YETTA JANKOWSKY (KAY), 23 September 1918, aged 69

5. EDITH CHARLES, 4 February 1920

6. JEANETTE ISAACS, 10 May 1920

7. LAWRENCE

8. FANNY ABRAHAMS, 6 October 1920, wife of late Lewis Abrahamson

9. ABRAHAM STEIN

10. ESTHER SILVERSTONE, 1 February 1922, aged 73, wife of Myer Silverstone

11. FANNY SAMUELS, 27 September 1922, aged 72

12. MARIA JACOBS, 7 October 1922, aged 84, relict of John Jacobs

13. PHOEBE BARKE, 26 June 1922, aged 77

Division Path

14. RACHEL BASH, 17 January 1924, aged 60, wife of the late Samuel Bash

15. ELIZA EMDON, 22 June 1924, age 75

16. SARAH SILVERSTONE, 29 January 1925, aged 75

17. SARAH LILIAN SIMMONS, 9 March 1926, aged 15

18. FANNY ABRAHAMS, 27 December 1925

19. MINNIE ISAACS, 3 April 1926

20. LEAH BURNS, 12 November 1929, aged 69

21. REBECCA CONICK, 27 April 1930, aged 63

22. ELIZABETH JACOBS, 1 June 1930, aged 73

23. BELLA EDELMAN, 3 June 1931, aged 63

Gap

30. ETTIE ASH, March 1964, aged 55 (née da Costa)

31. MISS DORIS BAUN, 12 December 1963, aged 62

32. ANNE LEVY, 4 April 1962, aged 47, wife of Herman Levy

33. BRONIA FELDMESSER-REISS, 25 January 1960, aged 61, born 30 April 1898

34. MRS AZERMAN

35. MAUD BRADLAW, 8 April 1957, aged 81, widow of Henry Jack Bradlaw [N35]

36. MRS PRICE, 19 March 1956

37. LEAH KERSCHENBAUM, 13 March 1955, aged 64, widow of Barnett Kerschenbaum

ROW O

1. ABRAHAM TITLEBAUM, 20 January 1927, aged 75

2. BENGIMAN JOSEPH, 28 January 1926, aged 61

3. AARON JOEL WEINBERG, 16 November 1912, aged 46

4. MARK JACOBS, 28 October 1913, aged 74, husband of Henrietta Jacobs

5. HUGH EMDON, 31 May 1914

6. JOSEPH LEAPMAN JACOBS, 29 June 1914, aged 76

7. AFROIM DAVID, 6 December 1914, aged 70

8. Unknown

9. HARRIS BROMBERG, 23 March 1916, aged 78

10. JOSEPH DAVIS, 3 March 1917

11. MOSES DAVID MEANDL, 27 April 1917

12. ISAAC PRICE, 21 September 1917

13. JOSEPH JACOBS, 12 November 1917, aged 60
Division Path

14. HARRY NELSON, 8 January 1918, aged 39

15. BENJAMIN ROTH, 11 January 1918, aged 75, husband of Bertha Roth

16. HARRY PHILLIPS, 2 April 1918 (war grave)

17. Unknown
18. JOHN JACOBS, 7 May 1918, aged 87
19. DOUBTFUL
20. MORDECAI SLAVINSKI, 1 November 1919, aged 13, son of Aaron & Rachel Slavinski
21. JOHN LITHMAN, 8 January 1919 (war grave)
22. MYER NYMAN (Pte Michael Burns), 2 February 1919, aged 18 (war grave)
23. ABRAM BERNSTEIN, 10 March 1919, aged 58
24. ALBERT STANLEY BRADLAW, 10 December 1959
25. GEORGE DEFRIES, 21 March 1946, aged 70
26. BARNETT KIRSCHENBAUM, 17 June 1946, aged 58
27. GOLDSTONE, 17 November 1946
28. ISRAEL LEVY, 8 April 1948, aged 79, husband of Amelia Levy
29. SUGAR, 1948
30. WOLFF, 18 December 1949
31. MR F. WALL, 9 May 1950
32. ARTHUR RALPH WALFORD, 7 June 1950
33. MASTER RONALD CARMONA, 25 January 1952
34. ALEXANDER WEMBURY, 7 September 1953, aged 63
35. MR HARRIS, 23 January 1957
36. AARON SPERLING, 4 April 1957, aged 68

ROW P

First plot has been left clear for drainage
2. BERTHA JOSEPH, 31 March 1952, aged 79, wife of F Joseph
3. HENRIETTA JACOBS, 25 November 1909, aged 63, wife of Mark Jacobs
4. LEAH SAMUELS, 19 November 1909

5. HENRIETTA BROCK, 3 January 1909, aged 79, wife of Lewis Brock

6. KATE JACOBS, died 6 January 1899, aged 55, wife of J.L Jacobs

7. DEBORAH ULLMAN, 3 April 1899, aged 62, widow of Wolfe Jacob Ullman

8. HANNAH NATHAN, 26 January 1901, aged 74

9. FANNIE GOLDBERG, 28 June 1901, wife of Joseph Goldberg

10. ESTHER NATHAN, 23 November 1902

11. REBECCA NATHAN, 19 November 1903, aged 79

12. HARRIET MORRIS, 7 August 1904, wife of Abraham Morris

13. RAINA TITLEBOAM, 20 May 1905, aged 53

14. ESTELLE LOVEGUARD, 15 September 1905

15. HENRIETTA COHEN, 18 October 1905, aged 49, wife of Abraham Cohen

16. JANE NATHAN, 2 November 1905

17. ESTHER LEVY, 12 February 1907, aged 26, wife of Philip Cohen of Manchester

18. NANCY NATHAN, 5 January 1908

19. JULIA HARRIET PEARL, 7 December 1908, aged 59

20. RACHEL SOLOMON, 23 March 1909, aged 22

21. BESSIE OWEN, 7 April 1909, aged 66

22. RACHEL FREEMAN, 15 July 1909

23. PHOEBE LEAH FRANKS, 27 October 1909, aged 67

24. ANNIE BROMBERG, 8 September 1928, aged 81

25. MARTHA LEAH WOOLF, 3 August 1891, aged 58, wife of late Henry Woolf

26. CAROLINE SMITH, 25 April 1933, aged 83

27. MRS CURTIS, 11 November 1940

28. LEAH MICHON, 12 July 1944

29. MRS E KETNERIDGE, 1945

30. MRS SCHOLMAN, 5 March 1948

31. LILY KINGDON, 23 October 1948

32. KITTY PURCELL, 19 March 1949

33. Unknown

34. DOROTHY BARNETT, 3 June 1954, aged 53

35. M. J BOSMAN, 8 August 1954

36. JULIA BROCK, 17 December 1954, aged 80

ROW Q

1. RABBI JACOB BARUCH ELLINSON, 8 February 1924, aged 82 (check location correct)

2. LEWIS BROCK, 24 July 1920, aged 83

3. ELIEZER DAVID LEMPERT, 26 September 1912, aged 28, son of Fruma & Saul Lempert

4. SIMON MILNER, 4 October 1911, husband of Beeny Milner

5. HUGH RALPH EMDEN, 31 May 1914, son of the late Eliezer and Telza Emden

6. GEORGE BROCK, 24 July 1897, aged 81

7. SAMUEL SAMUELS, 5 July 1899, aged 79

8. MICHAEL BASCH, 24 September 1899, aged 38, 'a dutiful son and brother'

9. ELEAZAR EMDON, 26 February 1900, aged 59

10. HAYMAN LIGHTERMAN, 23 August 1900, aged 43

11. Unknown

12. HENRY JACOBS, 16 September 1903, aged 86

13. JOHN SELIG NELSON, 6 March 1904, aged 71

14. ISAAC LEIPMAN, 10 August 1904

15. EDWARD BASCH, 6 November 1904

16. ABRAHAM MORRIS, 4 September 1905, aged 78

17. EPHRAIM BARKE, 14 May 1904, aged 58

18. JOSEPH GOLDBERG, 14 July 1907

19. NATHAN FREDMAN, drowned 8 June 1884, buried 29 June 1884

20. BORUCH JAFFE, 18 August 1907

21. LOUIS MICHAEL JACOBS, 30 November 1907, aged 29, husband of Sarah Jacobs

22. BENJAMIN S PIK, 11 March 1908

23. Unknown

24. HENRY BLUMENTHAL, 19 January 1911, son of Abraham and Leah Blumenthal of London

25. Unknown

26. Unknown

27. Unknown

28. GEORGE RALPH, 7 February 1877

29. SAMUEL WHITE, 1 April 1924

30. LAZARUS LADDEN, 5 July 1933, aged 18

31. WILLINGTON, 15 March 1937

32. GEORG KOVAES (KOOD), 31 January 1938, husband of Bertha who lost his young life on Alba which sank off St Ives on 31 January

33. EMANUEL SPERLING, 18 January 194, aged 59

34. RONNIE CASMONA, 24 January 1952, aged 15, born Malta

35. MARK LOUIS MICHAELS, 15 December 1961, of Torquay

36. GOLDSTEIN, 27 May 1960

37. MR BARRS

ROW AA

1: MATHILDA (MORRIS) DICKER, 16 July 1963

2: AARON BASH, 6 August 1963, only son of Rachel Bash

3: LESLIE MORRIS, 22 December 1963

4: DANNY (GOLDSTEIN) COHEN, 8 December 1964

5: CLARA HILL, 1 April 1966

6: RETA REBECCA MATTHEWS, 28 April 1976

7: PHILLIP LEVY, 9 December 1976

8: GOLDA LEAH RICHARDSON, 6 December 1977

9: ABRAHAM WEMBURY (WEINBERG), 2 January 1978

10: ELIZABETH ARANKA MARSDEN, 30 April 1978

11. CHARLES ROSE, August 1979

12. KITTY LUBELL, 28 December 1980

13. SARAH ANNIE HORTON, 14 June 1980

Large gap

20. NICOLA MARJORIE ZELDA ROBINS, 15 February 1965

21. VIVIENNE EMDON, 3 December 1962

ROW AB

1. ESTHER SPERLING, 24 June 1959

2: HENRY GOLD, 30 December 1959

3. PERCY LESKIN, 8 January 1960

4. Empty

5: HERMAN ELIAS COHEN, 16 December 1960

6: SARAH MARCHEVITZ, 18 January 1960

7: ARTHUR BRAND, 15 June 1960

8: CAPLE PECK, 18 December 1960

9: JENNIE PECK, 31 May 1961

10: JENNIE GREENBURGH, 5 May 1961

11. HYMAN ROSEMAN, 17 October 1961

12. PERCY ROSEMAN, 25 March 1962

13. MARIE SEGAL, 21 January 1963

14: LEON FRANK EMDON, 2 February 1963

15: MOSES MONTEFIORE COHEN, 11 February 1963
16: GEORGE (LAZUR) LAZARUS, 17 February 1963
17: ISSAC EDWARD BROMBERG, 19 April 1963
18: ALICE AGNES NELSON, 10 January 1965
19: ESTHER MELICAN, 26 February 1965
20: HYMAN WISEMAN, 6 April 1965
21: ESTHER PERLMUTTER, 25 November 1965

ROW AC
1: ETHEL GRACE ROBINS, 19 April 1963
2: SARAH ALOOF, 7 May 1964
3: LEAH BENCE, 17 May 1964
4: ROSE EMDON, 7 June 1954
5. LEAH CAPLAN, 9 February 1966
6. AUGUSTA SPARK, 25 June 1966
7: BEATRICE GORDON, 11 September 1966
8: ETTY ESTHER GREEN, 5 October 1966
9: SIM LAZARUS, 4 February 1967
10: ISIDORE JOSEPH, 28 February 1967
11: EVA FIELD, 28 June 1967
12: JOE ERLICH, 5 August 1967
13: ROSE OWEN, 1 February 1969
14: WOLFE STERNE, 2 April 1969
15: PHOEBE COHEN, 30 August 1969
16: REBECCA DEGGOTS, 13 December 1969
17: PHILIP ERLICH, 21 August 1970
18: MORRIS LESKIN, 11 March 1972
19: ESTHER ROSE BRAND, 8 December 1970
20: ANNIE DORA JOSEPH, 31 May 1971

ROW AD

1: DOROTHY EMDON, 1 February 1966

2: EMMANUEL KLIEFF, 4 February 1969

3: ISRAEL ROSEMAN, 15 May 1969

4: BELLE ERLICH, 8 July 1970

5. SIMON ROSEMAN, 23 August 1970

6: JEANNIE FREDMAN, 4 January 1886, aged 54

7: SAMUEL W. FREDMAN, 2 February 1971

8: LILY COHEN, 19 July 1972

9: MINNIE GREENBURGH, 28 March 1973

10: JULIAN (LEO) HARRIS, 16 July 1973

11: ROSE CAPLAN, May 1974

12: ADA SILVERSTONE, 28 December 1974

13: MORRIS RUTMAN, 14 April 1975

14: PAULINE JUNE JOSEPH, 10 July 1975

15: BETTIE GORDON, 27 August 1975

16. JOSEPH SALISBURY, 28 September 1975

17. ISRAEL ELIAS SHAW, 24 June 1976

18: BERT DEGGOTTS, 22 February 1977

19: DR MORDICI ELEAZER (MARK) GORDON, 6 May 1977

20. Unused

ROW AE

1. DORA HARRIS, 9 November 1972

2. ANNIE SARAH (ENA) ROSEMAN, 8 March 1975

3: PEGGY ROSE JOSEPH, 8 April 1977

4: JOSEPH GERALD JOSEPH, 21 September 1977

5: MORTON JULES DAVISON, 11 October 1977

6: RUBY FURGUSON, 23 February 1978

7: PERCY LIONEL COHEN, 29 April 1978
8: HETTIE MARIE NELSON, 1 August 1978
9: THELMA SOLOMON, 1 August 1978
10: EPHRAIM BENCE, 7 October 1978
11 RUTH ELSIE DOROTHY BROCK, 28 February 1979
12: GOLDA FACTOR, February 1980
13: FORTUNÉE MORDO, March 1980
14: HETTY COHEN, 20 May 1980
15. REBECCA SALISBURY, June 1980
16. JOSEPH DUBOVIE, December 1980
17. RALPH SEGAL, 5 July 1981
18. GERALD ROBINS, 19 July 1981
19. BERTHA HURST, 7 December 1981, aged 77
20. SIDNEY HURST, 10 November 1987, aged 85

ROW AF
1. BARNET PERLMUTTER, 20 July 1981, aged 90
2. EDNA SILVERSTONE, 24 January 1982
3. HARRY GREENBURGH, 6 March 1982, aged 92
4. LILY PEARL, 15 July 1982, aged 82
5. ARTHUR GOLDBERG, 29 December 1982
6. COLONEL ROY TELFER, 10 January 1983, aged 84
7. GERALD BUSTELL, 26 January 1983, aged 48
8. LOUISE SOLOMON, 17 May 1952 – 20 July 1993
9. SARAH LEWIS, 8 August 1983, aged 88
10. AIMEE ROSEMAN, 1896-1983
11. IRENE ROSEMAN, 16 March 1984, daughter of Aaron & Hinda Roseman

12. BERTRAM HARRIS EMDON, 17 January 1916 – 29 March 1984, aged 68
13. LAURA HARRIS, 15 July 1984
14. HERMAN HENRY COHEN, physician, 6 September 1984, aged 81
15. LILY WISEMAN, 1894-1984
16. JOHN BERTRAM GOODMAN, 5 October 1905 – 21 January 1985
17. DR HARRY GREENBURGH, 28 June 1917 – 28 March 1985
18. Empty?
19. HENRY PECK, 26 July 1985, aged 70, husband of Freda
20. LEAH ROSEMAN, 19 September 1985, aged 73

ROW AG

1. ISIDORE PERLMUTER, 18 October 1985, aged 69
2. RUBY HANNAH BEGLEMAN, 29 September 1986, wife of Jock
3. WOLFE (BILL) BLOOM, 16 May 1987, aged 85
4. ETTA BAS AARON HETTY ROSEMAN, 1897 – 1987, widow of late Simon Roseman
5. FRANCES SARAH LEWIS, 28 January 1925 – 25 May 1987
6. MARK BROCK, 20 April 1900 – 13 December 1987
7. ERNEST EMDON, 27 April 1914 – 25 May 1987
8. DOC SPIERS, 26 January 1988
9. ROSE BAUN, 15 February 1988, aged 91
10. ROSA HAZAN, 16 May 1989
11. BEATRICE COHEN, 6 March 1990, aged 93
12. HARRY HIRSHMAN, 6 July 1990, aged 81
13. ANN SOWDEN, 22 December 1933 – 28 December 1990
14. FREDA SARAH ROSEMAN, 4 February 1991, aged 86, daughter of Myer Isaac & Amelia Fredman
15. BERTHA SHAW, 26 April 1991

16. RUBY COHEN, 24 December 1991, aged 82, widow of Harry Cohen
17. MYER LADDEN, 30 December 1991, aged 86, son of Lewis & Janet Ladden
18. VIVIAN ABRAHAM ROBINS, 22 January 1992
19. BERTHA ROSEMAN, 31 January 1992, aged 80
20. LEAH (LILY) ALOOF, 12 December 1986

ROW AH

1. JACK COHEN, 1 August 2006, aged 94
2. Empty
3. Empty
4. ISRAEL GORDON, 24 October 2001
5. ROSE GORDON, 25 June 1997
6. BENJAMIN GREENBERG, 22 April 2005
7. MINNIE GREENBERG, 16 March 1997
8. PATRICIA LIPSON, 6 February 1997
9. LIONEL JOHN ALOOF, 5 August 1996
10. LEONARD MILLER, 1937 - 1995
11. EDWARD MARK EMDON, 26 April 1995
12. WLADIMIR BLEIER, 29 March 1995
13. LEILA ANNIE RUTMAN, 2 October 1994
14. HENRY ROY CAPLAN, 18 August 1994
15. LOUIS ROSEMAN, 13 April 1994
16. ETTY CANT, 31 August 1993
17. SIDNEY ALOOF, 9 April 1993
18. REVA ERLICH, 27 December 1992
19. EVE LOMAN (SOLOMON), 27 October 1992
20. EILEEN BEATRICE ROSEMAN, 22 March 1992

ROW AI

1. Empty
2. Empty
3. FAY 'PUDGE' SPIERS, 26 November 2007
4. DAVID JOSEPH RUTMAN, 20 August 2007
5. BETTY ROSS, 1 December 2006
6. BERNARD (BEN) HENRY LEVAN-HARRIS
7. SOLLY SOLOMON, 12 November 2006
8. SHEILA LEAH BRISK, 5 August 2005
9. PERCY ALOOF, 19 May 2003
10. CECIL LUI (SONNY) SILVERSTONE, 19 January 2002
11. HETTY SAMUEL, 1901 - 2002
12. MAX BRISK, 8 October 2001
13. BESSIE ALOOF, 5 August 2001
14. PHYLLIS THOMAS (MORRIS), 27 November 2000
15. LESLIE D. LIPSON, 16 June 2000
16. ANN DUBOVIE, 4 October 1999
17. MICHAEL ANTHONY SPIERS, 25 August 1999
18. WILLIAM (JACK) BEGLEMAN, 25 February 1999
19. VIOLET EVELYN, 24 December 1998
20. ROY SILVERSTONE, 23 June 1997

ROW AJ

1 -14. Empty
15. REVA HODES JOSEPH, 29 December 2001
16. RITA ROBINS, 10 July 2010
17. HANNAH (ANNE) ESTHER BENTLEY, 1919 - 2009
18. ALBERT JOSEPH PERLMUTTER, 17 March 2009
19. MILTON JACOBSON, 8 April 2008

20. MITZIE WINSTON, 8 December 2007

Rows AK & AL have no burials or tombstones as of August 2012

ROW BA

1: Hebrew only

2: RACHEL JACOBS, 27 December 1966

3. ISAAC TSINOWAY, 9 March 1967

4: ROSE FINE, 12 November 1967

5: BERNARD HYMAN GOODMAN, 7 January 1969

6: HARRY LEWIS, 18 May 1969

7. DIANA STADDON, 29 April 1974

8. Empty

ROW BB

1. Empty

2. HENRY CONYBEARE WOOLFSTEIN, 15 June 1969

3. ALF LAZARUS, 28 October 1985, aged 77

4. TOBY, mother of Jack, Jill, Elan, Daphne & Ari

5. SIDNEY COLLINS, 18 June 1990, aged 72

6. Empty

7. Empty

8. Empty

ROW BC

1- 4. Empty

5. VALENTINE GHZALA BATE, née Sillam

6. JOSEOH VARLEY (VASHAFSKI), 23 November 1912 – 24 August 1995

7. ISRAEL MARKS, 23 September 1995, aged 69

8. Empty

ROW BD

1. LEAH LEVY, 13 December 1995, aged 70

2. Empty

3. SAUL BERGER, 11 January 1998, aged 83

4. RACHEL HOUSE, 11 April 1936 – 1 March 2000

5. Empty

6. Empty

7. RACHEL COLLINS, 8 June 2008, aged 91, née Halperin

8. Empty

War Graves in the cemetery:
- John Lithman, late of the Judeans 38/40 Royal Fusiliers, died 8th January 1919 [5679] aged 16 years and 9 months, and in the Hebrew inscription mi-tzeva ha-yehudit (= from the Jewish Army). *He falsified his age to serve in the Jewish Battalion and died in some kind of accident.*
- Myer Nyman of Swansea who served under the name Pte Michael Burns, of the Jewish Battalion, died 2 February 1919 aged 18 years and 4 months.
- Stoker Harry Phillips of HMS Vivid, died 2 April 1918 aged 29.

Graves from the Second World War in this cemetery are:
- Sgt Ralph Emdon of the Queen's Royal Regiment who died 1944 of wounds received at Dunkirk

- Sgt Morris Solomon of the Royal Australian Air Force who died on 21 July 1942 aged 23.
- So too the deaths of the first civilian casualties in bombing on Plymouth are marked with a double grave – that of mother and daughter, Mary and Esther Smith, who died on 10 July 1940 as a result of a German bombing raid.

(Below) The double tombstone of Mary and Esther Smith, the first civilian casualties of the blitz on Plymouth in WW2

Jews' Cemetery Lodge, Plymouth

FURTHER READING

Berger, Doreen. *The Jewish Victorian: Genealogical Information from the Jewish Newspapers 1871-1880*, Robert Boyd Publications, 1999

Fry, Helen. *A History of the Exeter Jewish Community*, Halsgrove, 2013

Fry, Helen. *A History of the Plymouth Jewish Community*, Halsgrove, forthcoming 2014

Fry, Helen. *Jews in North Devon during the Second World War*, Halsgrove, 2005

Hidden Legacy Foundation. *The Jews of Devon and Cornwall*, Redcliffe Press, 2000

Jamilly, Edward. *The Georgian Synagogue: an architectural history*, Jewish Memorial Council, 1999

Kadish, Sharman. *The Synagogues of Britain and Ireland*, Yale University Press, 2011

Kadish, Sharman. *Jewish Heritage in England: An architectural Guide*, English Heritage, 2006

Pearce, Keith & Helen Fry (ed). *The Lost Jews of Cornwall*, Redcliffe, 2000

Roth, Cecil. *The Rise of Provincial Jewry*, 1950

Susser, Bernard. *The Jews of South-west England: The Rise and Decline of their Medieval and Modern Communities*, University of Exeter Press, 1993

THE AUTHOR

Historian and biographer Helen Fry has written over 23 books on the Second World War and aspects of Anglo-Jewish history. These include: *Churchill's German Army*; *Music and Men; Freuds' War, Jews in North Devon during WW2; Inside Nuremberg Prison* and *From Dachau to D-Day*. In fiction under the pseudonym JH Schryer she has co-written two novels: *Goodnight Vienna* and its sequel *Moonlight over Denmark*. Helen is currently writing film and TV scripts on some of her optioned works. She can be found on Facebook and Twitter. Her website: www.helen-fry.com

Printed in Great Britain
by Amazon